CHRIST-BASED LEADERSHIP

CHRIST-BASED LEADERSHIP

DAVID STARK

with GARY WILDE

BETHANYHOUSE
Minneapolis, Minnesota

Published by Bethany House Publishers
11400 Hampshire Avenue South
Bloomington, Minnesota 55438

Bethany House Publishers is a division of
Baker Publishing Group, Grand Rapids, Michigan.

Printed in the United States of America

Library of Congress Cataloging-in-Publication Data

Stark, David, 1955-
    Christ-based leadership : applying the Bible and today's best leadership models to become an effective leader / David Stark.
        p.   cm.
    Summary: "Christ-Based Leadership paints a portrait of Christian leadership within a biblical framework while comparing and contrasting it to today's hottest leadership tools"— Provided by publisher.
    Includes bibliographical references.
    ISBN 0-7642-0141-7 (hardback : alk. paper)
    1. Christian leadership. 2. Leadership—Biblical teaching. 3. Leadership—Religious aspects—Christianity. I. Title.
    BV652.1.S695   2005
    253—dc22   2005021038

To my wife, Janet, who has been my partner through this journey
of understanding God's vision of leadership.

To my mentors, who consistently acted differently than the norm.

To the business leaders who gave us their wisdom and
experience through their writing.

And finally, to the church.
My hope is that these ideas will take form and substance
in many congregations in the future
to the glory of God.

DAVID STARK is director of Changing Church Forum, a ministry of Prince of Peace Lutheran Church (*dave@changingchurch.org*) and president of BusinessKeys International (*dstark@businesskeys.com*). He divides his time among three roles: pastor, business consultant, and trainer. He is coauthor of *LifeKeys, LifeDirections,* and *Growing People Through Small Groups* and author of *Christ-Based Leadership* and his own small-group material, *People Together.* Stark holds a BA in biology and an MDiv from Princeton Theological Seminary. He and his family reside in Minneapolis.

CONTENTS

Are You Leadership Literate?

This book came to life in my spirit on an unforgettable day in the early 1990s as I was reading global forecaster Alvin Toffler's *The Third Wave*. Toffler had always been quite prescient about the future, and his well-known statement struck me to the core:

> *The illiterate of the 21st century will not be those who cannot read and write, but those who cannot learn, unlearn, and relearn.*[1]

At that time, well into my first years in ministry, I longed to learn the essence of good leadership. I also had a sneaking suspicion that I might need to unlearn and relearn a few things along the way. At any rate, energizing my quest were two different sets of motivations, each based on a leadership model.

The first bubbled up from my unsatisfying experiences with a certain model of small-group ministry. My senior pastor had asked me to apply it as soon as I arrived, and though I chafed at its top-down, authoritarian approach, I used the program "successfully" for a number of years.

Nevertheless, it was exhausting. What enormous effort just to sustain the leaders' vision! People weren't enjoying this, I wasn't enjoying it, and the fruit produced in participants' lives hardly resembled the fruit of the Spirit. Where was the love, the joy, the peace among us? We settled instead for much division, consistent strife, little unity, and feeble enthusiasm.

———————

I decided to look for a new way to do small-group ministry. While reading Toffler's book, it occurred to me that the business community, out of necessity, was moving into innovative structures to accomplish its goals in the work force. This secular marketplace movement, which was starting to look strangely similar to my own direction, was crucially based upon a deeper understanding of leadership. Could I learn from the business gurus while maintaining a thoroughly biblical philosophy of ministry? The idea intrigued me.

———————

Before I continue, please allow me a moment to review the basic thesis of *The Third Wave*. Toffler suggests that civilization has subsisted in three basic structures, or "waves," down through history.

The agricultural first wave involved living and laboring on extended family farms (which is still applicable for much of the world).

In the second wave, the industrial revolution, people began working in hierarchical organizations built around command-and-control models of leadership. The era of the machine was built upon mechanistic efficiency.

Then, around 1955, we entered the third wave: the information age. Here and now, Toffler says, a new working structure is evolving: less hierarchical, interdependent organizations that gather around communities of commitment. Peter Drucker would later call these "organic organizations," because *the master image is no longer the lifeless machine but the living organism.*

As I swam around in cutting-edge business thinking, one day it hit me: the *New Testament* uses the organic as its master image: the body of Christ. However, while we've had this theology of an organic organization from the beginning, the business community seemed to be moving from theory (its "theology") to application with more determination than the church.

This was out of necessity, of course, to meet the demands of a rapidly changing, swirling, exciting, startling world: Globalization. Computerization. Postmodernism and Gen Y. Talk radio, bloggers, and eBay. How else would they survive, thrive, and get their message across? Leaders in every field rose up . . . to lead. They tackled the problem on all fronts—they had to, for profits must not fall.

We, the church, on the other hand: Have our prophets fallen? It seemed to me we were holding on to second-wave forms of leadership and structure at all costs. We continued to create and maintain top-down, hierarchical, command-and-control, mechanistic organizations. Sound at all like your church?

That very day I committed myself to reading and digesting as much of the business revolution material as I could find. I drilled far into insights about effective leadership and people-empowering structures. I wanted to learn, in full detail, what it would mean to lead an organic organization. And I figured I had an advantage: My organization is indwelt by the Spirit of God himself.

HOW DO YOU VIEW YOUR WORLD?

The more I read business literature, the more I saw two profoundly distinct schools of leadership thought. In his wonderful book *Leading Change,* James O'Toole describes this worldview conflict; the first is the *Realist-relativist-contingency* school, which holds the following assumptions about the world and people (and therefore leadership):

- People are by nature evil and self-interested, thus they must be controlled;

- Human groups are given to anarchy;

- Progress comes from discipline, order, and obeying tradition;

- Order arises from leadership;

- There can only be one leader of a group;

- The leader is the dominant member of the group;

- Leadership is an exercise of power;

- Any sign of weakness will undercut the leader's authority;

- Loyalty, effort, and change can be commanded successfully.[2]

O'Toole spends several chapters showing that this view doesn't work in the long run because it's an amoral leadership style that harbors a built-in self-destructiveness:

Leaders in the Realist School are prone, when pressed by the inevitable exigencies of public life, to behave in ways that destroy the trust of followers. Because people will not follow the lead of those they mistrust, contingency leaders will often encounter insurmountable obstacles on the road to leading change.[3]

By contrast, *Rushmorean* leaders have remarkably different assumptions about the world and people. "Rushmorean" refers to the character and values of people like Washington, Jefferson, Lincoln, and Roosevelt. They possess authenticity, integrity, vision, passion, conviction, and courage, and they lead by example rather than coercion. Rushmorean leadership is moral leadership, and its axioms would read:

- People are by nature a mixture of potential for great good or great harm, and they thrive in an environment of trust with accountability.

- Human groups tend toward self-ordering states, given the right parameters and resources.

- Progress comes from vision and values given as parameters, where self-discipline, creativity, and passion are allowed to stretch people forward.

- Order arises from common commitments to mission and common understandings of values.

- There are many types of leadership and leaders within an organization.

- Different leadership energies are needed at different times to keep an organization moving to its prime.

- Leadership is an exercise of stewardship, where everyone shoulders the trust given to the organization.

- Weakness and vulnerability on teams create an atmosphere of trust, where members feel needed for their strengths as well as needing others for the areas where they do not have strengths.

In this approach, everyone involved buys into any change effort as members together craft a common vision out of various agendas. In this way they capture the best future for the organization and take advantage of the stakeholders' diverse gifts and passions. As Toffler puts it:

No leader can command or compel change. Change comes about when followers themselves desire it and seek it. Hence the role of the leader is to enlist the participation of others as leaders of the effort. That is the sum and essence not only of leading change but also of good management in general. In reality, such leadership is extremely difficult because it is unnatural.[4]

As I reflected on these contrasting paradigms regarding the world, people, and leadership, I came back to one of Jesus' clearest statements. He too lifted up a basic leadership contrast—the difference between leadership that reflects God's kingdom and leadership that works against His purposes in the world.

"You know that the rulers of the Gentiles lord it over them, and their high officials exercise authority over them. Not so with

you. Instead, whoever wants to become great among you must be your servant, and whoever wants to be first must be your slave—just as the Son of Man did not come to be served, but to serve, and to give his life as a ransom for many."
MATTHEW 20:25–28

Peter reinforces Christ's words when writing to early church leaders:

To the elders among you, I appeal as a fellow elder, a witness of Christ's sufferings and one who also will share in the glory to be revealed: Be shepherds of God's flock that is under your care, serving as overseers—not because you must, but because you are willing, as God wants you to be; not greedy for money, but eager to serve; not lording it over those entrusted to you, but being examples to the flock. And when the Chief Shepherd appears, you will receive the crown of glory that will never fade away.
1 PETER 5:1–4

I began to see that the New Testament establishes a crystal-clear difference between leadership that "lords it over others" and leadership that proceeds from the Holy Spirit to build the kingdom. How similar to James O'Toole's Realist/Rushmorean distinction! In fact, how similar to everything I'd been reading in the business revolutionaries, those who knew that "business as usual" must radically alter its approach in order to impact its world.

I was inspired by and excited about the possibilities. I also thought, *Wouldn't it be great to have a book that shows how scriptural truths can work hand in hand with the best insights of business research?*

That's what *Christ-Based Leadership* hopes to do. We'll explore in detail the differences between these leadership types, launching into each theme from a pivotal question appearing in each chapter title. The questions will drive to the core of what today's leaders must be asking themselves in order to choose between the pathways open to them. Each chapter will also compare the components of leadership to the human body, showing by way of analogy the "look" of health or disease in the organic organization.

A TALE OF TWO WISDOMS

Recall that I had *two* motivations energizing my quest for excellent leadership. If the first was solidly intellectual, the second was much more emotional and spiritual in nature. In the years that followed, as I began working as a church consultant, I constantly observed amoral-leadership assumptions working themselves out within congregations.

The result? Pain!

Lots of pain was being created in the church, manifesting in all kinds of ways. I could broadly categorize the hurt in three forms of woundedness:

(1) *Missed opportunities for laypeople to live out their gifted-ness and callings. They ended up in disillusionment and often rejected the institutional church as a place of fulfilling their life's purpose.*

(2) *Hurt, confused, abused, and stifled staffers and layleaders. These folks wanted to give their best to their leaders, but found the amoral leadership patterns hindering and obstructive at least, offensive and destructive at worst.*

(3) *Divided and diminished congregations. Within their communities, they never had the impact they were designed to have.*

Alongside such painful situations, though, I encountered hope-inducing examples of moral leadership in action. These leaders had the opposite effect on laypeople, staffers, and congregations. *Where is all the pain?* I wondered at first. Then I realized how very different the assumptions about people and the world were in these healthy scenarios. They blossomed with vitality and ministry, bringing glory to God in myriad ways. There is something irrefutably wise about working within Christ's body as if it were an organic organization. Which, of course, it is!

Here, then, were two very different "wisdoms," those of which the apostle James spoke long ago:

> *Who is wise and understanding among you? Let him show it by his good life, by deeds done in the humility that comes from wisdom. But if you harbor bitter envy and selfish ambition in your hearts, do not boast about it or deny the truth. Such "wisdom" does not come down from heaven but is earthly, unspiritual, of the devil. For where you have envy and selfish ambition, there you find disorder and every evil practice. But the wisdom that comes from heaven is first of all pure; then peace-loving, considerate, submissive, full of mercy and good fruit, impartial and sincere. Peacemakers who sow in peace raise a harvest of righteousness.*
> JAMES 3:13–18

In each chapter ahead, while considering a key question about effective leadership, we'll look at (1) the biblical wisdom supporting the principle involved and (2) the specific business theory it upholds. Get ready to enjoy "mini-book reviews" of pivotal volumes; those you don't yet own may end up on your bookshelves eventually. My hope is that churches will begin applying these wonderful principles, along with their moral bases and structural implications. If this can ease and eliminate some of the pain caused by unbiblical, hierarchical leadership patterns, I will be deeply gratified and grateful to God.

THE TIME IS RIPE!

Before jumping ahead, let's return for a moment to *Leading Change*. After his extended treatment of moral leadership, James

O'Toole spends the remainder of the book asking, "Why hasn't this type of change happened yet?" Given its moral integrity and its demonstrated real-life effectiveness, why is it so hard to find? After raising many possible answers, he finally comments:

> In all instances in modern society, then, change is exceptional. When it comes about, it does so primarily as a response to outside forces. It may also occasionally occur through shifts in values—say, as a result of social learning "when the time is ripe." And most rarely, it may come about as the result of leadership. But in no case does it come about readily.[5]

Given the difficulty of the practical task before us, I want to suggest that now may be exactly the right time for such change to happen (even though it surely *won't* come about readily). Here's why:

First, we've arrived at a crossroads, where church leadership must change in order to *respond to new spiritual elements in American culture*. When the business community began its transformation, increased competition and globalization meant companies could no longer be product-driven; they had to become market-driven and niche-sensitive. Similarly, the church no longer has a monopoly on what people consider spiritual: We now compete against many other ways of meaning-making in postmodern culture. Therefore, out of necessity, we must learn how to embrace multiple people-niches and people-needs with targeted ministries.

Second, the time is ripe not only because we must adapt to change but also because we must *take up our divinely bestowed stewardship more responsibly*. Jeffrey Hollender reflects upon the sense of stewardship seen in the corporate social responsibility movement unfolding around the world:

> Take a walk through any airport, and take a look at the business books. They're all about teamwork and cooperation and making the firm more like a family. Look at the way the

stakeholder concept is taking hold, all over the world, which is truly a triumph of cooperation over competition. . . .

As we as a society undergo this profound shift in the conventional wisdom . . . we're entering into a debate that involves every institution in society evolving over time, from government to private enterprise to the church and the press. We tend to assume that the world is pretty much the way it was when we were born, but in fact it is not true. Look at the enormous speed of change as people have begun to redefine the roles of virtually every institution we know of.[6]

Moral leadership is no longer an isolated set of ideas based upon a biblical worldview; we don't have "the market" to ourselves. Instead, it is necessary for all peoples, for all coming generations, to learn to care for one another and for the gifts we've all been given. If even the most secular business leaders believe this, how can church leaders bypass it?

Third, the time is ripe because of the *growing reality of global interconnectedness.* At this writing, the lead article in *The Economist* praises the Internet's triumph in giving power to the consumer. The Net, however, is merely the biggest symbol of a connectivity that occurs in countless ways today. Our financial markets are interconnected, our security is interconnected, and we are also environmentally interconnected as never before. Accordingly, this is an age in which no organization, including the church, can hide itself from the others.

To conclude with a biblical image, we might reach back to Genesis and recall the whole world uniting under one language at the Tower of Babel, just as we today have done online. What happened *then*? God intervened and confused human communication because "if as one people speaking the same language they have begun to do this, then nothing they plan to do will be impossible for them" (11:6). In other words, being interconnected and communicative does carry substantial risk, and if we choose to use such blessings wrongfully, God will not permit it to endure.

By contrast, suppose we seek His will, humbly, in *all* that we do—in every form of relationship, communication, structure, and ministry?

One thing I know: Ours is a time when moral leadership must lead our organizations. I hope you will be inspired by this same vision as you turn the pages ahead. As you face the challenges of learning ... unlearning ... relearning, I also hope you will quickly find ways to join with others in embracing and applying this New Testament leadership model right where you live and minister. The time is ripe for all of us.

—David Stark
Summer 2005

O N E

What Is the Truth of Your Ambition?

As an interested observer, I saw it clearly: *He's ambitious.* I watched as one of his associates tossed out a teasing jest, "Hey, I just heard they're thinking of calling you to _____ Church" (naming one of the largest, most prestigious churches in the U.S.). This senior pastor, then leading a much smaller congregation, nearly leapt out of his chair with excitement.

Only to be quickly deflated. "Just kidding, brother," he heard.

In that moment I witnessed a soul unveiled, a man whose drive for recognition and power lay at the center of his life. And what happened in his church, on a daily basis, was a crime. Staff members became emotionally and spiritually sick, often leaving the ministry completely. Leadership meetings swirled with conflict and crisis, people sensing that important decisions had already been locked in at clandestine gatherings behind the scenes.

When he did take his next step up the ecclesiastical ladder, I experienced firsthand how such leadership destroys congregations. Within weeks of his departure, all the pent-up anger, shame, and woundedness came bubbling to the surface. Therapy practices filled to capacity with hurting members. Many of them no longer attend any church to this day.

Not a pretty sight, is it.

Thankfully, it doesn't have to be like this. Because the leadership styles of pastors and layleaders have profound impact—for good or for ill—they're back on the map these days. One of the central renewal movements of the past decade has been Bill Hybels' Leadership Summit, sponsored through the Willow Creek Association. Tens of thousands of pastors, staff members, and volunteers have attended to drink in the wisdom of leaders from a wide variety of fields.

I'm one of them. And one of my favorites over the years has been Jim Collins, author of *Built to Last* and *Good to Great: Why Some Companies Make the Leap . . . and Others Don't*. A self-proclaimed seeker, Jim had long been reluctant to deal with the topic of leadership because he believed that "poor leadership" had become a too-convenient catch phrase. Businesspeople would fall back on it whenever anything went wrong, thereby escaping a close look at functions and processes, avoiding candid scrutiny of areas calling for positive change.

As he consulted with companies, therefore, Jim asked his staff not to include leadership as a criterion for the movement from good to great. However, his crew wouldn't take no for an answer; the data kept pointing to this critical area of organizational life. What finally pulled Jim over the line was the type of leadership he saw in companies that outperformed the whole marketplace in moving from a good company to a great company. He called this "Level 5 leadership."

Why Level 5? Because this style forms the fifth rung of a developmental ladder that great leaders always seem to reach.

Jim also stuck with "Level 5" to avoid any other common descriptors that might diminish what for him is a crucial tension to maintain: the paradoxical nature of a leader's behavior at this level, that between *personal humility* and *professional will*. In Jim's research studies, Level 5 leaders maintained a healthy balance between the two.

In contrast, the Level 4 leader usually had a large ego that set up a company for future failure, and, overall, Level 4s just didn't perform as well. To paraphrase Jim Collins from his book *Good to*

Great, here are some important characteristics of Level 5s:

- They are ambitious, for sure, but first and foremost for the company.

- They display a compelling modesty, are self-effacing and understated.

- They are fanatically driven, infected with an incurable need to produce results.

- They display a workmanlike diligence, more of a plow horse than a show horse.

- They look out the window and attribute success to something other than themselves.

- They look in the mirror when something goes wrong, take responsibility, and blame themselves.

Think about it: Can you cultivate this type of leadership?

LEVEL 5   **LEVEL 5 EXECUTIVE**
Builds enduring greatness through a paradoxical blend of personal humility and professional will.

LEVEL 4   **EFFECTIVE LEADER**
Catalyzes commitment to and vigorous pursuit of a clear and compelling vision, stimulating higher performance standards.

LEVEL 3   **COMPETENT MANAGER**
Organizes people and resources toward the effective and efficient pursuit of predetermined objectives.

LEVEL 2   **CONTRIBUTING TEAM MEMBER**
Contributes individual capabilities to the achievement of group objectives and works effectively with others in a group setting.

LEVEL 1   **HIGHLY CAPABLE INDIVIDUAL**
Makes productive contributions through talent, knowledge, skills, and good work habits.

Jim Collins, *Good to Great* (HarperCollins, 2001), p. 20. Used by permission.

You may have ascertained that how you answer has much to do with what's inside—the essential *you*. In fact, when Jim Collins presented this material on the day I sat spellbound before him, he ended with the one big question that makes all the difference between Level 4 and Level 5 leaders: *"What is the truth of your ambition?"*

CALLING ALL GOOD SHEPHERDS!

Sit with that question for a moment, as I did. Let it sink down deep into your heart. When Jim asked it, he was entering into a theme that wafts through the Bible from beginning to end. I immediately think of the direct command in Philippians 2:3, where Paul writes: "Do nothing out of selfish ambition or vain conceit, but in humility consider others better than yourselves." A much longer Old Testament passage shows what ambition can do to leadership. In Ezekiel 34, we find the prophet rebuking those who merely take care of themselves; focused solely on their own goals, they failed to look after the people God had placed into their hands.

The word of the LORD *came to me: "Son of man, prophesy against the shepherds of Israel; prophesy and say to them: 'This is what the Sovereign* LORD *says: Woe to the shepherds of Israel who only take care of themselves! Should not shepherds take care of the flock? You eat the curds, clothe yourselves with the wool and slaughter the choice animals, but you do not take care of the flock. You have not strengthened the weak or healed the sick or bound up the injured. You have not brought back the strays or searched for the lost. You have ruled them harshly and brutally. So they were scattered because there was no shepherd, and when they were scattered they became food for all the wild animals. My sheep wandered over all the mountains and on every high hill. They were scattered over the whole earth, and no one searched or looked for them.*

"'Therefore, you shepherds, hear the word of the LORD: *As*

surely as I live, declares the Sovereign LORD, *because my flock lacks a shepherd and so has been plundered and has become food for all the wild animals, and because my shepherds did not search for my flock but cared for themselves rather than for my flock, therefore, O shepherds, hear the word of the* LORD: *This is what the Sovereign* LORD *says: I am against the shepherds and will hold them accountable for my flock. I will remove them from tending the flock so that the shepherds can no longer feed themselves. I will rescue my flock from their mouths, and it will no longer be food for them.'"*

vv. 1–10

What happens to the sheep who experience such shepherding? Ezekiel later speaks of what's going on with the people:

As for you, my flock, this is what the Sovereign LORD *says: I will judge between one sheep and another, and between rams and goats. Is it not enough for you to feed on the good pasture? Must you also trample the rest of your pasture with your feet? Is it not enough for you to drink clear water? Must you also muddy the rest with your feet? Must my flock feed on what you have trampled and drink what you have muddied with your feet?*

34:17–19

When leadership focuses on its own ambition and gain rather than on organizational health or mission, we find the sheep (employees, staff, volunteers)

- being harshly treated under the leader;

- resorting to "turf wars," competing for resources;

- leaving the organization, at a loss for leadership;

- becoming fair game for "wild animals," forces that can destroy their (spiritual) lives.

Sadly, while this type of leadership is common in the church today, it is ever-so-subtle and rarely recognized, consciously, by the one wielding the power.

Recall the ambitious senior pastor whose story opened this chapter. If he had encountered Jim Collins' question ("What is the truth of your ambition?"), he'd have given a beautiful, theologically correct, mission-driven, kingdom-focused response . . . yet his actions would betray his words. Jesus said, "By their fruit you will recognize them" (Matthew 7:20).

There's a better way. I think of another pastor, another church with a happier story that has one of the largest and most successful ministries in its niche. Its leader demonstrates an ideal balance of personal humility and professional will, often giving statements like, "I don't aspire to greatness, but I do hope to influence those who will be great in the church."

The staff around him experiences empowerment, fair treatment, and a sense of his authentic desire to see the advancement of God's kingdom. In ten years, this church has spawned dozens of new pastors, hundreds of missionary trips, and multiplied its ministry among several congregations throughout the nation. The pastor told me once that he'd had to create a form letter for turning down all the churches constantly contacting him to take a position with them.

Remember that because the church is a body—the body of Christ—we can feel the impact of certain leadership attributes if we imagine how they might be experienced in a physical human body. Suppose, for instance, that selfish ambition were at the core of a physical body. Then the head would only take care of itself, hardly giving a thought to what was happening with the toes or shoulder blades, doing only what brought its own pleasure or development, "eating" only what pleased the mind, leaving the stomach begging for nourishment. If intellectual exercise were the only game in town, the leg muscles might begin complaining of weakness—or worse. In time, the whole body would become sick, unable to function, facing its own self-destruction.

I recently watched a documentary depicting this scenario in widescreen Technicolor. *Super Size Me,* billing itself as a film of "epic portions," has a simple plot. Director, writer, and leading man Morgan Spurlock set out to answer an intriguing question: "What would happen if I ate at McDonald's, and only McDonald's, for a solid month?" He would do no exercise, take no vitamins or supplements, and eat at McDonald's ninety times in thirty days.

Several doctors examined him before his experiment and found him to be in excellent physical shape for his age. Their predictions? They thought his triglyceride levels would rise a little, but in only a month's time not much else would occur.

They were dead wrong. His triglyceride and cholesterol levels shot up to dangerous levels in just a few days. He gained over twenty-five pounds and began having heart palpitations, night sweats, and symptoms of depression. His liver began functioning like that of an alcoholic, with his internist begging him to stop at day fifteen, lest he "fry" that essential organ.

Of course, Spurlock thought he *liked* fast food. But when the head only eats what satisfies itself, refusing to care for the rest of the body, a deadly dis-ease permeates the whole. This happens, too, when leadership focuses only on its own ambition. The subsequent toxicity amid those who follow is surprising. Shocking. Greater than most people would ever predict.

COMPARING AND CONTRASTING LEVEL 4 AND LEVEL 5 LEADERSHIP

Because I certainly don't want to depress you, let's flip to the positive side and see what's so great about Level 5 leadership. To paraphrase Jim Collins from his book *Good to Great,* here are some important characteristics of Level 5s:[1] It could be pictured as a person pursuing a healthy diet, exercising regularly, doing whatever strengthens and nurtures the body—personal care for optimum function. Level 5 leadership has health-inducing effects; when leaders care for their people and their mission, organization-wide healthy dynamics result. Staff members are treated fairly and feel empowered. Employees and laypeople are excited and proud to be part of the whole. *The body functions well.*

The three "health charts" below compare and contrast the Level 4 and Level 5 leaders in three areas, respectively: overall personality qualities, impact on staff persons, and effect on laypeople.

WHAT DO WE SEE IN THEM?

Level 4 leadership	*Level 5 leadership*
Need to be right, others wrong	Take appropriate blame and responsibility for their actions
Can't apologize or admit their mistakes	Will admit their mistakes and assume that no one is perfect
See political gamesmanship as an appropriate tool to get what they want	Understand that appropriate processes are an important check and balance to their vision and leadership
Lie easily, find scapegoats, and blame others	Tell the truth, even when it reflects badly on them or causes a setback for the organization
Afraid of others' ideas and may reframe them into their own	Open to others' ideas and will quickly give credit where it's due
Tend to be inauthentic, as if wearing a mask	Exude an authenticity that garners trust
Central messages are law-based; everyone must measure up to their standard	Central messages are grace-filled; everyone is accepted and challenged to stretch further

HOW DOES THE STAFF EXPERIENCE THEM?

Staff experience under Level 4 leadership	Staff experience under Level 5 leadership
Treated unfairly; leader's agenda dominates decision-making	Treated fairly; mission and values dominate decision-making
Spend lots of energy defending or trying to acquire authority they already should have	Spend lots of energy developing the ministry through their appropriately delegated authority
Work in a heavy, exhausting, and guarded atmosphere of distrust	Work in a trusting, open, joyful, fun, and energizing atmosphere
Struggle not to gossip, get angry, or form alliances for productivity	Look forward to what the staff team can accomplish together
Feel blamed, criticized, shamed, or even sick when interacting with senior leadership	Feel accepted, valued, encouraged, appreciated when interacting with senior leadership

WHAT DO LAYPEOPLE PICK UP?

Layleaders under Level 4 leadership	Layleaders under Level 5 leadership
Receive messages stating: You're unacceptable where you are; admonished to measure up	Receive messages stating: You're accepted where you are; invited to grow
Feel "in the way," not important to the organization's central work	Feel cared for and included, ministered to, central to the organization's mission
Pulled into taking sides amid internal battles with staff and leadership	Experience support and trust among the staff
Leave the organization confused, hurt, and relieved to be out of its influence	Leave the organization changed in a positive, exciting way

A word of caution as you use these to consider your organization's health. Most leaders aren't living solely within one sphere or the other; most have multiple motivations and often vary their styles. However, if you see most or many of the symptoms of ambition-centered leadership, realize that change *is* needed. Like a person who eats junk food nonstop, an organization can sicken and languish in depression. The situation will need to be addressed; concerned leaders and members *must* act. Wisely, gently, over time—and perhaps with the help of professional consulting—they can enter a planned, systematic change process that listens to everyone's voice.

At this point, you may be saying, "But David, are you telling me I've got to remove all ambition from my heart and make my motives perfectly pure before God can use me?"

Not at all! I love the way Frederick Buechner puts it in *The Magnificent Defeat:*

The voice that we hear over our shoulders never says, "First be sure that your motives are pure and selfless and then follow me." If it did, then we could none of us follow. So when later the voice says, "Take up your cross and follow me," at least part of what is meant by "cross" is our realization that we are seldom any less than nine parts fake. Yet our feet can insist on answering him anyway, and on we go, step after step, mile after mile. How far? How far? [2]

We can go right to Jesus to calm our fears about any ambition-centeredness we discover within us. Jesus wasn't afraid of strong leaders who dealt with ambition—He chose two to be His disciples. In a somewhat humorous text, we find the mother of James and John trying to secure the best seats in heaven for her ambitious sons:

The mother of Zebedee's sons came to Jesus with her sons and, kneeling down, asked a favor of him. "What is it you want?" he asked. She said, "Grant that one of these two sons of mine may sit at your right and the other at your left in your kingdom."

"You don't know what you are asking," Jesus said to them. "Can you drink the cup I am going to drink? "We can," they answered.

Jesus said to them, "You will indeed drink from my cup, but to sit at my right or left is not for me to grant. These places belong to those for whom they have been prepared by my Father."

When the ten heard about this, they were indignant with the two brothers. Jesus called them together and said, "You know that the rulers of the Gentiles lord it over them, and their high officials exercise authority over them. Not so with you. Instead, whoever wants to become great among you must be your servant, and whoever wants to be first must be your slave—just as the Son of Man did not come to be served, but to

serve, and to give his life as a ransom for many."
MATTHEW 20:20–28

It's not ego strength that Jesus denounces; in fact, He utilizes that in some cases to accomplish, through us, the great tasks ahead. Rather, *He takes this ambition and gives it a completely different channel:* "If you want to be great (read: 'If your desire has been for selfish ambition'), then become a servant of all." *We can legitimately strive for stardom in service.*

Makes sense, doesn't it? Why would it be wrong to want to be great for God and His kingdom?

Even so, be aware that it's a vastly different matter to build our own kingdom for our own glory. God wants to work with natural human motivation and turn it toward its proper end—which, in a delicious paradox, will end up being more fulfilling for us anyway. It's about how we *apply* all of this energy within us, this deep desire for success that beats so mightily within our chests.

CHALLENGING THE CULTURE MODELS

If you've done any study in this area as a Christian leader, I'm sure you realize that not all current cultural (or marketplace) wisdom on leadership aligns with God's call to us. Some secular models fly in the face of what He desires for the church; these will do little to take a good church down the pathway to greatness, or they may even completely obstruct the Spirit's work in this process. That's why Jesus says we are sheep among wolves, that we must be wise as serpents and innocent as doves.

Jim Collins' research can help bolster our resolve *not* to follow such models. This is not an easy stand to take, and there are plenty of twists to throw us off track. Yes, great organizations exercise Level 5 leadership, but . . .

The great irony is that the animus and personal ambition that often drive people to positions of power stand at odds with the humility required for Level 5 Leadership. When you combine that irony with the fact that boards of directors frequently operate under the false belief that they need to hire a larger-than-life, egocentric leader to make an organization great, you can quickly see why Level 5 Leaders rarely appear at the top of our institutions (Jim Collins, Good to Great (Harper Collins, 2001), pp. 36–37. Used by permission).

Does this give you cause for pause about the kind of leaders you want in your church? Does it call you to carefully analyze the models—and the role models—you're using in ministry? Good! Because great Christian leadership will often depart drastically from current cultural norms and expectations. The famous servant text of Philippians 2 is worth quoting here as the Lord's role model of "humility on a mission":

Your attitude should be the same as that of Christ Jesus:
Who, being in very nature God,
Did not consider equality with God something to be grasped,
but made himself nothing,
Taking the very nature of a servant,
being made in human likeness.
And being found in appearance as a man,
he humbled himself
and became obedient to death—
even death on a cross!
Therefore God exalted him to the highest place
and gave him the name that is above every name,
that at the name of Jesus every knee should bow,
in heaven and on earth and under the earth,
and every tongue confess that Jesus Christ is Lord,
to the glory of God the Father.
    vv. 5–11

In light of such declarations—and the ultimate example of our Lord himself—why do we persist in our self-centered leadership? I'd like to suggest three of the most common reasons. We might call them pitfalls, traps into which we hurtle headlong when we're not paying attention to leadership qualities. Then we fail to challenge the predominant cultural models; we let the selfish-ambition aspects of our leaders slip by.

WE TRIP OVER THE "ARGUMENT FROM STYLE"

Some leaders offer a seductive excuse for not challenging their ambition-centered tendencies. The argument goes like this:

> *Hey, everybody's different, right? People's personalities and spiritual gifts cause them to exercise very different leadership styles too. Some are naturally more autocratic and some are more collaborative. There are models of both types in the Scriptures. Just think of the differences between Moses and Joshua, for example. A broad spectrum of leadership styles have been at work throughout the history of God's dealing with His people. And God uses a variety of styles and methods to accomplish His purposes, since organizations, like people, differ greatly. So . . . back off!*

As a certified Myers-Briggs Type Indicator practitioner, and as one who has helped thousands of people with their personal styles, I understand and agree with much of this argument. Yes, people are different, and God does use a wide variety of styles to accomplish His purposes. However, *personal style is never an acceptable excuse for poor behavior.*

Let's take an instance from the world of personality types. If I have a creative personality that doesn't easily handle the idea of being on time for meetings, I'm not justified if I persist in being late—I must adjust my behavior in order to be considerate of others. Similarly, if a leader's personality style and ego strength typically cause her to get right to the point, she doesn't have a free ticket to insensitivity or rudeness. She must lay her personality open to the Spirit's transforming work; over time she can grow in love and compassion through His influence.

WE SUCCUMB TO THE APPARENT AUTHORITY OF A GIFT

It's true that some people have the spiritual gift of leadership or administration. This can get in our way, though, especially if it allows for a disconnect between what a leader preaches and how he acts. My gift of leadership doesn't let me opt out of planning, collaborating, and working together with other members of Christ's body (even though it may help me do these things more effectively). We are all to use our gifts in mutual edification, building one another up in the Lord.

One of my mentors in ministry was a man of great confidence and ego strength, an outstanding communicator. He told me that faith and hope were always easy for him, but that love was his cutting-edge growing point.

Throughout his career, he suffered many broken relationships and was constantly making amends because of this struggle with his default way of relating to people. Nevertheless, as he allowed God to work in him, he gradually became a more loving person. The irony and wonder of his journey is this: If you met him today, you would say he is one of the most gentle, loving men you've ever known. As he would put it, this is "power perfected in weakness." God has had to come through in his life where he was not naturally strong, and he has become a much more effective leader as a result.

WE FALL TO A FALSE JUSTIFICATION

What a horrible reason to allow selfish ambition in our leaders: The end justifies the means. We don't usually put it that starkly, however—we have ways of making it seem okay. For example:

Well, I know God has called me to lead this organization, and I'm confident about the vision and the direction we need to travel together. As I look at the various players here, though, I see potential blockers in a few leadership circles of influence within the congregation. Therefore, I need to plan effective political moves that will neutralize their influence, so we'll end up in the place where God wants us to be. We do want to be where He wants us, right?

Sadly, this approach usually leads to actions that are less than above-board and much less than Christlike.

Once again, there is *some* truth here: God does give His chosen leaders vision and direction, and certain pockets of people in any congregation "just aren't there yet." Some will even directly and vehemently oppose what God wants to accomplish in a church. However, the fruit that springs from using inappropriate means will so spoil a church culture that even if the goal is accomplished, the toll in wounded human souls is hardly worth it. The very atmosphere will reek with spoilage.

Remember Abram and Sarai's decision to take God's promise into their own hands? Since He had long delayed in providing them a child, they decided to procreate through a surrogate mother, Hagar.

> *Now Sarai, Abram's wife, had borne him no children. But she had an Egyptian maidservant named Hagar; so she said to Abram, "The LORD has kept me from having children. Go, sleep with my maidservant; perhaps I can build a family through her."*
> GENESIS 16:1–2

Notice three things about this text.

First, Sarai blames God for the apparent failure. Often this is an unspoken assumption of leaders who want to justify inappropriate means of leadership: God should have removed, or somehow changed, those who are blocking our church's direction!

Second, Sarai crafts a clandestine alternative to "help God out." But can we indeed help God? Will He truly be pleased with the shady means we offer for accomplishing His goals?

Third, Sarai justifies her scheming by highlighting the hoped-for outcome: She'll be able to build a family. Isn't that a noble and appropriate aim?

This third element gives us the most trouble—our vision of the marvelous and lofty goal, the desired end. It often lets us sweep under the rug any second thoughts we might have about the means. Not long ago I was consulting with a church in which I saw this type of behavior up close. "Pastor Bob" and his leadership team were trying to decide among three alternatives for the future direction of their congregation. Should they build a new facility on site? Should they create a satellite site nearby? Or should they simply plant a new, self-supporting congregation on the other side of town?

All three alternatives seemed good, and Pastor Bob was having his staff (along with several congregational representatives) weigh the pros and cons of each. The problem was that he'd already made up his mind to build; he wasn't open to planting a church or creating a satellite situation, but he didn't communicate that to any staff or elected leaders while he continued to lead a yearlong, well-orchestrated process of discernment.

When the time came to put the alternatives up for a vote, everyone was feeling positive about the prayerful and lively debate. Rather than trusting God along with the leaders around him, though, Pastor Bob decided to make sure his desired outcome came to pass.

Just before the night of the ballot, he met with one of his most influential layleaders and cemented a plan. Two minutes before the vote, Pastor Bob would announce that he wasn't open to any alternative but erecting a new building. Then, on cue, the layleader would say: "Well, that settles the matter. Are there any questions?"

Needless to say, trust was broken. The building was built, but the staff struggled for years to genuinely trust one another. As I interviewed associate pastors later, I found that they didn't want to reconnect with this staff after they left the church. The charade and the end-around had left them feeling disrespected and valued only for their functions, not their place on the team.

It happens all the time. We think the end will justify the means. We forget that our Lord is more than the God-of-the-Big-Picture; He is God-of-the-Process too. It matters *that* we do the right thing, and it matters *how* we do the right thing.

Time and time again, we see the God of the Scriptures conveying unique and specific plans related to the *means* of leadership. Our challenge is to trust. To trust that the Almighty is well able to accomplish, with appropriate means, the vision He gives to His people.

TAKING THE FIRST STEPS TO LEVEL 5

We're called to practice humility-in-determination. This is our sanctified ambition, our energetic hungering to serve, our aspiration to be great in servanthood. It will never be a call to passivity or tentative response; it's a full-throttled, warmhearted attachment to God's own priorities. We know that "He must become greater; I must become less" (John 3:30). So we go for it!

If you'd like a better balance between professional will and personal humility in your own leadership style, consider first a few practical steps:

(1) *Begin focusing on the mission of the organization more than your own personal advancement. God uses strong leaders who do so.*

(2) *Allow a group of people to be independent of your direct control. Let them hold you accountable with genuine consequences, and make sure they're folks who won't just give you the answers you want to hear.*

(3) *Give your staff members an anonymous mechanism for providing feedback. Let them say how they view the center of your ambition. Have someone other than them summarize and give you this feedback periodically.*

Can the elected layleaders take some steps too? Yes. They can help put safeguards in place, creating checks and balances for leadership. Here are starter suggestions along these lines for maximizing your organization's health:

(1) Don't allow control of the finance committee, personnel committee, and nominating committee to reside in the central leaders' hands.

(2) Do regular reviews with the senior leadership, including appropriate professional developmental plans.

(3) Set missional goals and targets from which all ideas can be considered.

(4) Put developmental plans in place for other members of the staff.

(5) Form a group of people who can hear the concerns of layleaders and staff. Make sure they can share safely about any problems or needs. Give this group the appropriate authority to challenge and hold accountable the senior leadership.

I hope you've picked up on the obvious deficiencies of Level 4 leadership. It's an approach that dissipates potential for healthy growth by turning all energy inward. It enmeshes the poor sheep in turf battles and territorial defense schemes, or it forces them into constant recovery mode due to harsh treatment. Then the only outward energy flowing from a congregation comes from the ones leaving the flock altogether.

Let it not be! Today's congregations must go boldly into their communities to attract people to faith, making great leadership increasingly important. Thankfully, Level 5 leading will help focus the whole organization outward, for just as the prophet Ezekiel told us long ago, much of the energy of a shepherd after God's heart reaches outward in seeking the lost and bringing back the strays, strengthening the weak and binding the wounded. What a blessed sight when this happens in our midst.

I want to challenge you to carry Jim Collins' question in your heart: "What is the truth of your ambition?" If we can be leaders who are highly motivated but also humble in our approach and behavior, we can lead our organizations from goodness to greatness with God's blessing.

FOR REFLECTION

Use this space to write down your reflections, reactions, insights, and responses to this chapter and its central question.

What is the truth of my ambition?

T W O

Who Is Lord of Your Leadership?

Here's a quick brainteaser for you: How much can Jesus do?
    Well, let's see . . .

. . . *He can create the stars and planets, fling the galaxies far and wide,*
travel light-years in a flash . . .
. . . *He can move a mountain from here to there, destroy a temple and*
build it again in three days, make a blind man see . . .
. . . *He can preach and teach, melt the human heart, bring the strong-*
est to their knees, and cast out devils . . .
. . . *He can make a child feel worthy, comfort the grieving, raise the*
dead, and even guarantee paradise to the worst sinner . . .

I know, but suppose we ask Jesus himself? "I can," He says, "do
nothing. . . ."

NOTHING, WITHOUT ANOTHER

That's right. Neither Jesus nor we can do anything . . . *on our*
own. The Scriptures support the idea. Among the most discussed
New Testament texts, for instance, is the "kenosis passage" of Philippians 2:5–7:

*Have this attitude in yourselves which was also in Christ Jesus,
who, although He existed in the form of God, did not regard
equality with God a thing to be grasped, but emptied Himself,
taking the form of a bond-servant, being made in the likeness of
men.*

NASB

The word for "emptied" in the Greek text is *ekenôsen,* and Bible scholars have long debated of what, exactly, Jesus emptied himself when He became flesh. We know He freely laid aside the full expression of His heavenly glory while on earth; we also know that He also chose to hold at bay, to a great extent, the full exercise of His divine power.

However, I see another way—a most profound and instructive way for us—in which Jesus emptied himself. *He willingly chose not to know in advance* all the specifics of His life, work, and mission while among us. Yes, because of the Holy Spirit's input, He certainly developed a clear picture of these things early in His ministry. But that is my point: While on earth, Jesus came to depend upon the Spirit to guide and lead Him in all He was to accomplish. "The Son can do nothing by himself," He said.

Jesus emptied himself in this way, I'd like to suggest, because He wanted to give His followers a clear and shining example. "This is your model," He says in effect. "Here's how a Spirit-guided life actually looks in daily living." See how clearly this comes through in John's gospel:

*So, because Jesus was doing these things on the Sabbath, the
Jews persecuted him. Jesus said to them, "My Father is always
at his work to this very day, and I, too, am working."*

*For this reason the Jews tried all the harder to kill him; not
only was he breaking the Sabbath, but he was even calling God
his own Father, making himself equal with God.*

*Jesus gave them this answer: "I tell you the truth, the Son
can do nothing by himself; he can do only what he sees his*

Father doing, because whatever the Father does the Son also
does. For the Father loves the Son and shows him all he does.
Yes, to your amazement he will show him even greater things
than these."
    5:16–20, EMPHASIS ADDED

Catch that? *Everything Jesus does relates to what the Father is*
doing. All of the Son's activity flows from the Spirit's guidance as
the Father directs. A perfect Trinity of interdependence.

So what do we see, for example, when Jesus hears that His
friend Lazarus lies deathly ill?

Jesus loved Martha and her sister and Lazarus. Yet when he
heard that Lazarus was sick, he stayed where he was two more
days.
    JOHN 11:5–6

Jesus waits. The disciples, awash in confusion, simply can't
understand the blessed pattern that characterizes a Spirit-discerning
life:

A life event occurs.
A withdrawal to quietness, discerning the Spirit . . .
A time of waiting in God's presence . . .
A time to act.

Jesus stays away for two days and then tells the disciples they
are now to go to Lazarus. They still don't see what God is doing,
so Jesus tells them plainly that Lazarus is dead, but that what's
about to happen is for the purpose of helping them believe.

Those of us who've served as pastors or layleaders can relate to
the anger and hurt of Martha and Mary, sisters of Lazarus. *Jesus*
didn't come right away! Why? Nevertheless, if it was Jesus' practice
to wait upon the Holy Spirit in all things, couldn't Martha, Mary—
you and I—learn to do the same?

Then Jesus looked up and said, "Father, I thank you that you have heard me. I knew that you always hear me, but I said this for the benefit of the people standing here, that they may believe that you sent me."

When he had said this, Jesus called in a loud voice, "Lazarus, come out!"

The dead man came out, his hands and feet wrapped with strips of linen, and a cloth around his face. Jesus said to them, "Take off the grave clothes and let him go."

JOHN 11:42–44

In this short passage, we get a glimpse behind the scenes. Jesus had been talking with His Father the whole time. Now He simply utters aloud a snippet of the conversation for the benefit of all observers (including us). *This ongoing conversation is to be the pattern of our own lives, day by day.*

THE WAY FOR *US* TOO?

You may be protesting: "Okay, *obviously* Jesus was led by the Spirit during His whole time on earth. But is this really normative for our twenty-first-century lives—for believers *today*?"

This completely legitimate question points us elsewhere in the New Testament for exploration: (1) the *words* in the gospel of John, where Jesus introduces the Spirit to the disciples, and (2) the *actions* of these disciples in the book of Acts. There we see them responding repeatedly to the Holy Spirit's leading in discernment, guidance, and direction.

IMPORTANT WORDS: AN INDWELLING WITHOUT TIME LIMITS

In John 13:31–17:26 we find the last discourse of Jesus. These are some of the final—and therefore extremely important—words He spoke to His disciples (and to His Father) before He went to the cross. Many topics arise in this section, but one major purpose is Jesus' desire to introduce the Holy Spirit in detail to the disciples.

Why did He spend so much time teaching about the Spirit at this juncture? Consider: He is soon leaving them physically; He plans to keep leading them spiritually; the indwelling Holy Spirit will be their Leader; they must know this Spirit and learn to follow Him. It's as if Jesus is saying, "This isn't a total good-bye, gentlemen. I'll still be with you, but in a different way. I want you to fully understand that way and thereby learn to live within its blessings. Prepare yourselves for this marvelous change of lifestyle."

Simply put, His followers needed to know what they could expect the Spirit to do *after* Jesus ascended to heaven—from that time forward *to the present day*. Here are some of His mind-blowing words, which we too can take directly to heart:

> *"I will ask the Father, and he will give you another Counselor to be with you forever—the Spirit of truth. The world cannot accept him, because it neither sees him nor knows him. But you know him, for he lives with you and will be in you. I will not leave you as orphans; I will come to you."*
>
> 14:16–18

> *"The Counselor, the Holy Spirit, whom the Father will send in my name, will teach you all things and will remind you of everything I have said to you."*
>
> v. 26

> *"You are my friends if you do what I command. I no longer call you servants, because a servant does not know his master's business. Instead, I have called you friends, for everything that I learned from my Father I have made known to you."*
>
> 15:14–15

> *"I have much more to say to you, more than you can now bear. But when he, the Spirit of truth, comes, he will guide you into all truth. He will not speak on his own; he will speak only what*

he hears, and he will tell you what is yet to come. He will bring glory to me by taking from what is mine and making it known to you. All that belongs to the Father is mine. That is why I said the Spirit will take from what is mine and make it known to you."
16:12–15

The Holy Spirit will lead the disciples by listening to Jesus and making known to them what Jesus asks Him to make known. The Spirit will remind them of everything Jesus had said and will communicate to them things still to come. In other words, the very way Jesus has been relating to the Father in the Gospels (by listening to the Holy Spirit and responding) is exactly the way *they* will live after Jesus has ascended to heaven.

And if they do indeed live this way? They, and *we*, have this promise: "I tell you the truth, anyone who has faith in me will do what I have been doing. He will do even greater things than these, because I am going to the Father" (14:12).

SIGNIFICANT ACTIONS: A GROUP OF FOLLOWERS WITH COURAGE

With Jesus no longer at their side, the early believers must have faced wrenching discouragement—initially, at least. However, eventually they recalled His wondrous promise to be with them through the indwelling presence of His Spirit. Again, the disciples live this out in the most practical ways throughout Acts; in fact, this biblical book comes to us as a virtual study manual on how to follow the Spirit's leading. We see . . .

■ Peter being led to Cornelius's house;

■ Paul being led to Ephesus;

■ Philip being led to the Ethiopian eunuch;

■ Ananias being led to heal Paul's eyes;

■ Agabus being led to take a collection for Jerusalem.

There is not space in this book to lay out all the specifics of how God guides us. (This is done more thoroughly in *Life Directions,* which I coauthored with Jane Kise.)[1] Here, I'll simply state the key point for leadership: *The indwelling Holy Spirit calls to the heart of every Christian leader: "Respond, moment by moment, to My leading."*

BEWARE THE DEADENING DISCONNECT

Do we hear that gentle call? Do we respond to those inner whisperings? Is the Spirit saying anything to you at the moment? Have you taken time to listen today?

Let's return to the body analogy we explored in the previous chapter. If we all are the body of Christ, under Jesus, the one Head, then it follows that our leadership unfolds in response to what the Head of our body is communicating and directing us to do. If our leadership does not do this . . . look out!

We know some of the most debilitating human diseases involve nerves that are no longer responding as the brain directs: for example, multiple sclerosis, Parkinson's disease, Tourette's syndrome. A similar disconnect can occur in Christian leadership. Sometimes a leader, even with the best of intentions, is no longer seeking or responding to direction. This creates, even amidst flourishing activity, organizations that are cut off from the purpose and work that God would accomplish in and through them.

I watched it happen. During the dot-com years of the nineties, I kept tabs on one organization that rocketed from a value of $250,000 (the initial capital investment) to millions in a just a few short years. The leaders of CompuWidgett.com were dedicated Christians who met weekly for Bible study and prayer. I enjoyed seeing them revel in the excitement of building a showcase enterprise in the new economy. Times were good.

When the chance to "go public" finally arrived, Fred, the CEO, prayed hard about CompuWidgett's future. So many possibilities! He knew a friend from his college days, Jack, who might be interested in buying. *Is that what you want, Lord?* Fred kept asking.

Fred would be attending a college class reunion in two weeks, so he prayed, "God, if I'm even going to consider an offer from Jack, two things need to happen. First, Jack has to attend this reunion. Second, you'll need to give us a chance to be alone so I can fully explain the opportunity."

Fred headed to the reunion with a peaceful heart . . . and there was Jack! They were indeed able to talk in private for a couple of hours. The result: an offer from Jack of $100 million—*four hundred times* the startup cost. Fred came home knowing that God had answered his prayers to the max.

The problem? Fred didn't *really* take that leading to heart. I know this because he promptly let the rest of CompuWidgett's leadership team convince him the company was worth a lot more than Jack's offer. So they wheeled-and-dealed, bargained here and there, held out for top dollar.

Until times weren't so good anymore.

Until CompuWidgett began looking like the hundreds of other sky-rocketing enterprises now sinking into dot-com oblivion. The company never went public. Instead, it suffered massive layoffs as all the leaders left for other opportunities and loads of investor money swirled down the drain.

Here's the sad part: How far could $100 million go if invested wisely in the kingdom of heaven?

How many hungry children could be fed?

How many hospitals or schools could be built?

How many churches could be planted?

How many Bibles distributed?

How many missions expanded?

How many . . . (add your own vision here)?

Yet Fred's own pride, and the motivations of those around him, caused CompuWidgett to veer off course and miss countless heavenly opportunities.

On the other hand, I know many great stories of Christian leaders in the church and in business faithfully responding to God's leading. Recently, in Minneapolis, when we sponsored a faith and business conference with other area organizations, one CEO sat on a panel that was addressing this point.

"I have a special closet in my office at work," he said. "I call it my prayer closet. When my company faces major decisions, I go to that closet by myself, get down on my knees, and ask Jesus what He would have me do."

By his own admission, he doesn't always get it right. But he very much wants to respond to the Spirit's guidance in his leadership.

LETTING THE LORD LEAD

How do you become this kind of Spirit-responsive leader? It's a matter of taking steps—very small ones in the beginning.

The *first* step is to allow God to become Lord of your leadership. Please realize: anyone who's moving in that direction will tell you it's a process of spiritual growth, of being trained to discern the Spirit's voice through many different inputs—interacting with God in all circumstances, seeing Him at work in every event, meeting Him within every moment. The great writer and cleric Henri Nouwen spoke of this often.

> *To pray, I think, does not mean to think about God in contrast to thinking about other things, or to spend time with God instead of spending time with other people. Rather, it means* to think and live in the presence of God. *Praying is not an isolated activity; it takes place in the midst of all things and affairs that keep us active.*[2]

Learning to live in God's presence, becoming skillful at this "discerning skill," doesn't happen quickly. As with training to excel at a sport or with an instrument, it takes practice and commitment to want to be led by God. By commitment, I mean that it may involve some painful waiting, some learning of patience, and a definite willingness to let God work according to His own timing, even if you're just dying to leap ahead. Are you learning to live with this "sacred tension"? Theologian Ronald Rolheiser says:

> It is good to carry tension and not resolve it prematurely because, ultimately, that is what respect means. By not demanding that our tensions be resolved we let others be themselves, we let God be God, and gift be gift. . . . if only [we] would not panic and resolve the painful tensions within our lives too prematurely, but rather stay with them long enough, until those tensions are transformed and help give birth to what is most noble inside us—compassion, forgiveness, and love.[3]

God is doing such birthing within each of us, all the time. It is our job simply to clear the way, to let it happen, because it's His work (and He does it quite well). I've noticed a common starting point in the stories I hear from Christian leaders about responding to the lordship of Christ. It begins with a solid decision that, in turn, works a major change of perspective: "I now freely acknowledge that *this* organization (company, church, or ministry) is no longer *my* organization; it's *God's* organization."

A friend of mine was the second-generation CEO of a family-owned company. His father had built a well-known and established entity that my friend took over after successfully building his own independent business. During his devotional time, a few years into this position, he sensed God asking him, "John, whose company is your company?" John remembers being perfectly honest in response: "God, I am letting you guide the decisions in my private life and in my family life, but I can handle the company by myself." Once again, God impressed upon him the same question: "Who is the ultimate leader of this organization, John?"

At that moment, John decided to allow God to be the company's leader. From that point on, slowly but surely, he learned to give control to his Lord. Two steps forward, one step back. But the process was unfolding; John was letting go.

This is typical of the first step of allowing God to be Lord of your leadership. It's a subtle movement of the soul, a shift in the heart, a slight loosening of the grip on your future. Eventually, this throws the floodgates wide open to blessing, and, significantly, there's no more "life engineering!" In most of the stories, I know there's a definitive and memorable beginning of some kind, but the initial decision has to be made over and over again, each day.

The *second* step toward becoming a Spirit-responsive leader usually includes small attempts in beginning to actually practice this process of giving over lordship. One group of professional executive women began to pray and study together, seeking to discover how their faith and business ventures might intersect. After exploring the ways God guides us, the leader challenged them to pray, at least once in the next month, for God to "use them or direct them in their day-to-day work world."

Chris took the challenge and on several mornings started her day with "God, if you want to use me this day, I am open to your leading." When the monthly meeting came around and the leader asked for sharing, Chris said, "I did pray, multiple times, that if God wanted to use me this day, I was open. Each time I lifted up that prayer, God used me significantly on that day."

She then frowned with concern and asked, "How far is this thing going to *go*?" Chris had experienced the excitement—the sometimes anxious thrill—of God directing her day in significant ways.

Part of this step involves seeing all of your life as a canvas upon which God paints His special callings, His whisperings to you. Sometimes even the apparent distractions are important, because they too can be the knock-knock-knocking of God on your heart's door . . .

The partitioning of life splits prayer and living, God and us.
When we consider "distractions" those things that are not pious
or religious, we are not letting God be for us in all of our lives.
We could almost say there is no such thing as a "distraction" in

prayer, but merely the experience of God providing the agenda.[4]

As we learn to let God set the agenda, we'll find it helpful to keep delving into Bible study to learn more about how guidance works in the life of a believer. Jane Kise's *Finding and Following God's Will*[5] is an excellent source to help you start (or continue) recognizing and following God's daily promptings. I offer the chart below as an all-too-brief summary of key concepts:

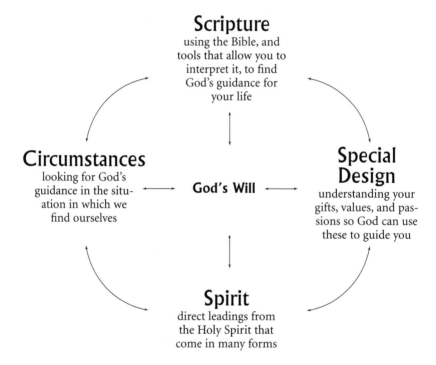

Scripture
using the Bible, and tools that allow you to interpret it, to find God's guidance for your life

Circumstances
looking for God's guidance in the situation in which we find ourselves

God's Will

Special Design
understanding your gifts, values, and passions so God can use these to guide you

Spirit
direct leadings from the Holy Spirit that come in many forms

You can take a *third* important step of practicing God's lordship in your life: Begin praying through the appointments of your day, asking for His input or guidance. *Lord, what would you have me say in this meeting? How would you like me to handle the conflict over here, the decision over there? What are you doing in this group, or directing for that one?*

Asking such questions with an open heart before God can work wonders. If nothing else, you enjoy the peace-inducing effect of knowing that your meetings are bathed in prayer. But, in fact, you matter to God—all of you and all of your requests matter to Him. Therefore, your vocational concerns are also of divine concern; why shut Him out of prime real estate in your inner landscape?

By describing this process in terms of steps, I'm saying that certain daily and weekly habits can begin to give real-time, real-life content to what Jesus as Lord of our leadership looks like. And as our faith deepens and matures, God allows our responsibilities to grow. That's why the *fourth* step in developing a lordship leader typically goes in a different direction: As we grow in sensitivity and responsiveness to the Spirit's leading, we'll find that we need more and more help from trusted people. We'll gather around us folks who can assist in discerning about tough or complicated situations that we face. God has placed us in those scenarios because we're ready for them and we'll meet them in collaboration with His wisdom.

Most stories I hear about leadership involve not only *individual* guidance but also *corporate* guidance. Again, we see this modeled by the apostles in Acts 15. The council of Jerusalem gathered to decide whether circumcision and obedience to the law should be required of all Christians, Jew and Gentile. These concerns were so central to the emerging church that the Spirit worked with its leaders to help resolve the issues. Similarly, in our time, important decisions require the perspectives of other leaders who also are focused on letting God be the Lord of their organizations. One of my best friends is a Christian leader who's wired quite differently than I am. I've gone to him as a sounding board at crucial times when I needed a perspective beyond my unique view of the world. *All* of us occasionally need this.

BE A CLOCK BUILDER

These patterns in a leader ultimately intersect with an interesting find from Jim Collins and his research team. Their first book looked at the leadership patterns of visionary and prevailing companies: Why did they keep succeeding over the long haul? *Built to Last* begins by describing the nature of their leadership, and Collins suggests that both the Myth of the Great Idea (you don't need to have one right away) and the Myth of the Charismatic Leader (you don't need to be one) do *not* define long-lasting organizations.[6]

So what does make the big difference? Leaders who act as clock builders. These leaders focus on setting up *processes*—"clockworks"—that allow their organizations to *keep on creating visionary products and leaders, decade after decade.* That clock keeps ticking, keeps creating, keeps expanding; it never runs down. Such long-term companies could be described like this:

- They focus on building great organizations (more than on money or fame).

- They value underlying processes (over one breakthrough idea).

- They sustain an atmosphere in which many successful leaders emerge (not just one charismatic leader).

So how does clock building connect to "allowing God to guide my leadership"? As Christians allow the Lord to guide, direct, and influence their leadership, two things will happen.

LONGEVITY DEVELOPMENT

God often puts processes in place that allow the organization to survive long after the clock builders have moved out of leadership. Biblical examples abound, but one of the best comes through in Exodus 18, where Jethro comes to visit his son-in-law, Moses.

"So, Moses," Jethro says, "how are things going for you?"

Moses then describes a huge problem. He's been doing what a typical charismatic leader might do to run an organization: He solves all the problems himself. In response, Jethro suggests a better way:

"What you are doing is not good. You and these people who come to you will only wear yourselves out. The work is too heavy for you; you cannot handle it alone.

Listen now to me and I will give you some advice, and may God be with you. . . . Select capable men from all the people—men who fear God, trustworthy men who hate dishonest gain—and appoint them as officials over thousands, hundreds, fifties and tens. Have them serve as judges for the people at all times, but have them bring every difficult case to you; the simple cases they can decide themselves. That will make your load lighter, because they will share it with you."

vv. 17–22

Clock building! Moses *creates processes* involving groups of tens, fifties, hundreds, and thousands. These processes will do their work far beyond his term of leadership, after Joshua takes over the nation.

For a New Testament equivalent, look again at the instructions in the book of Acts for building churches. Look too at the Pauline letters, telling us how the body of Christ is to function. Thousands of years later, God is still guiding us on how to build an organization and community that can last until Jesus returns.

SPECIFICITY DEPLOYMENT

God will show Spirit-responsive leaders both the strengths and limitations of their leadership. More and more, a leader will see where he should put his energies and where he should let others take over. He has certain gifts; others have complementary gifts. He learns to take charge and also to give away power—whatever is appropriate in any given situation. Moses (by his sin and, I would argue, his style of leadership) was *not* the one to lead the charge into the Promised Land, and the leadership mantle passed to the perfect candidate for that task: General Joshua. David was *not* the one to construct the temple; his son Solomon was the better fit for that project. Paul and Apollos, both committed Christian leaders, nevertheless had different roles in spreading the Good News:

What, after all, is Apollos? And what is Paul? Only servants, through whom you came to believe—as the Lord has assigned to each his task. I planted the seed, Apollos watered it, but God made it grow. So neither he who plants nor he who waters is anything, but only God, who makes things grow. The man who plants and the man who waters have one purpose, and each will be rewarded according to his own labor. For we are God's fellow workers; you are God's field, God's building.

1 CORINTHIANS 3:5–9

Notice that Paul, allowing God to be Lord of his leadership, advances the perspective that *all leaders are part of what God is doing*. God does value each of these men's roles and will reward each for his labor; Paul simply knows that both are fellow workers and servants of the Lord, who assigns the tasks. This firm sense of being-on-assignment rests deep within the heart of every surrendered Christian leader.

THE CRITICAL TEST: CAN YOU LET GO?

Is God the Lord of your work? You can tell by considering whether you're able to let go at the right time, whether you can peacefully allow Him to lift up a different leader to take over where you have finished.

Story after story of great Christian leaders tell us of their sense that "God has given me these tasks . . . for a time." They seem to know that He'll orchestrate just how long and how far they are to stay at the helm. When a leader thinks, *This is* my *organization,* he tends to overstay his heavenly invitation.

I went up close and personal with one such organization and its leader. This visionary entrepreneur, widely appreciated and respected, began a company that soon became internationally known for a particular ministry within churches.

Then it came time for him to begin transitioning the organization to a new group of leaders. Ouch! He burned through eight executive directors in eight years. He just couldn't allow God to be his leadership Lord. Consequently, the organization fell behind the curve and stopped responding to changing ministry needs. Within a year of his departure, his company was sold and dismantled. After thirty years of bringing new life and renewal to churches across the country, the company died a premature death because its leadership said no when God was saying, "Let Me orchestrate your future."

Any leader's heart can change. To quote the opening line of Rick Warren's *The Purpose-Driven Life,* "It's not about you!" Leaders who allow Christ to be Lord of their leadership know this in the depth of their being. God will use them powerfully, for a time, to lead the organizations they're building, but He will eventually connect that leadership to others. These new leaders will follow and take the organization into its next season.

I was mentored by Bruce Larson, whom I met when he had just taken over University Presbyterian Church in Seattle. A series of able leaders had built the church to fifteen hundred adult members, including a large college ministry. Over the decade that Bruce was senior pastor, they grew in size to over four thousand members before he left to pastor the staff at the Crystal Cathedral.

Bruce used to tell me he wanted to get off the platform before the leadership of the church *asked* him to get off the platform. This was his way of saying, "God is Lord of this church, and I will serve only as long as He asks." This attitude allowed the church's leaders to call Earl Palmer to follow Bruce and build America's largest PC/USA church.

Earl is a very different leader than Bruce, but God knew who needed to follow in order to build a lasting organization. I believe the church's growth could easily have been hindered had Bruce refused God's lordship of his leadership.

But what do *you* believe? The twenty-first-century church faces a culture increasingly apathetic—and sometimes downright hostile—to "organized religion." In this environment, won't our responsiveness to lordship become more and more crucial? Surely if the church is to meet its new challenges, it must stay in close touch with the Spirit's leading. *God is Lord of the church in all ages.* Nevertheless, in the awesome paradox of divine humility, He stands waiting for us to look to Him. He lets us make our decisions while continuing to gently call, pointing us to the blessed and fearful truth: "Unless the LORD builds the house, its builders labor in vain" (Psalm 127:1).

So I leave you with this second question: "Who is lord of your leadership?" Have you decided yet? If you have, how often do you genuinely pray for God's daily, work-related guidance and direction? These critical steps are foundational for Christian leaders if our organizations are to keep reflecting His vision and purposes among us.

FOR REFLECTION

Use this space to write down your reflections, reactions, insights, and responses to this chapter and its central question.

Who is lord of my leadership?

THREE

Do You Believe in the People You're Leading?

Over and over again, in times of change and renewal, the church has returned to the book of Acts to recall how it all began. Delving into those marvelous pages, we rehearse our sacred history. We gain insight and inspiration as we watch the Holy Spirit form and fashion the first generation of a radical new entity. One story in particular has recently grabbed my attention: the delegating of ministry to the first deacons.

In those days when the number of disciples was increasing, the Grecian Jews among them complained against the Hebraic Jews because their widows were being overlooked in the daily distribution of food. So the Twelve gathered all the disciples together and said, "It would not be right for us to neglect the ministry of the word of God in order to wait on tables. Brothers, choose seven men from among you who are known to be full of the Spirit and wisdom. We will turn this responsibility over to them and will give our attention to prayer and the ministry of the word."

This proposal pleased the whole group. They chose Stephen, a man full of faith and of the Holy Spirit; also Philip, Procorus, Nicanor, Timon, Parmenas, and Nicolas from Antioch, a convert to Judaism. They presented these men to the apostles, who prayed and laid their hands on them.

So the word of God spread. The number of disciples in Jeru-
salem increased rapidly, and a large number of priests became
obedient to the faith.

6:1–7

A problem arises in the growing fellowship. The disciples face a potential crisis. Look at the progression they follow to a solution:

- They uncover the exact nature of the problem.

- They reconfirm their priorities, given their gifts, callings, and limitations.

- They acknowledge a need for help from those of certain gifts and character.

- They identify a group of people with the right qualities.

- They lay hands on these people to delegate authority.

- They pray for the success of these people's ministry.

- They enjoy the result: explosive growth.

Love abounded in the early church. Members grew close and learned to trust one another deeply. Therefore, the disciples felt free to delegate crucial tasks to capable people around them; if they hadn't trusted these new *diakonoi* ("servants"), they would have tried to do all the work themselves, which would have quickly burned them out. Worse, it would have hindered or halted the church's expansion. Why? Because the disciples would have been sidetracked from using their central gifts. They were called to preach and pray; that is exactly what they needed to do, with single-minded focus. Others were needed for the meeting of practical needs.

If you don't think this decision was highly unusual, consider the context. Think about the major "management models" available at the time: Caesar's imperious, iron-fisted emperorship; local rulers in league with foreign powers; the Jews' own decidedly hierarchical Sanhedrin, which was particularly fresh in the minds of two disciples:

> *The priests and the captain of the temple guard and the Sadducees came up to Peter and John while they were speaking to the people. They were greatly disturbed because the apostles were teaching the people and proclaiming in Jesus the resurrection of the dead. They seized Peter and John, and because it was evening, they put them in jail until the next day. But many who heard the message believed, and the number of men grew to about five thousand.*
>
> *The next day the rulers, elders and teachers of the law met in Jerusalem. Annas the high priest was there, and so were Caiaphas, John, Alexander and the other men of the high priest's family. They had Peter and John brought before them and began to question them: "By what power or what name did you do this?"*
>
> ACTS 4:1–7

As we read on, we realize how profoundly the church's explosive growth threatened the religious authorities. The Sanhedrin meets to consider: How can we control this phenomenon without alienating all our people? Theirs is an organizational process centered on fear, supported by control and compliance. Joachim Jeremias describes exactly what the Sanhedrin had become in Jesus' time:

> *The New Testament attests this nepotism of the new hierarchy in a passage . . . Acts 4:5–6 . . . that the new hierarchy filled all the chief influential positions in the Temple with their own relations as a matter of course. Not only was the son-in-law of the former high priest Annas the reigning high priest, and his son captain of the Temple, but the ruling house of Annas had others, and perhaps all, of the chief-priestly positions in its*

control. The strength of this power the new hierarchy had taken to itself, whereby they controlled not only the Temple, the cultus, the priestly court, a considerable number of seats in the highest governing body, the Sanhedrin, but also the political leadership of the whole nation.[1]

Thankfully, it's not often that we see this much centralized power in our churches or organizations today. The point, though, is that *fear-based and control-based management processes hinder growth*, at times even aggressively attacking and destroying organizational expansion and health. Conversely, an organization with processes and leadership systems built on *trust within accountable boundaries* will likely flourish. Moving, in effect, from Acts 4 into Acts 6 is a good thing.

CONTRASTING DYNAMICS: CONTROL OR TRUST?

The Individualized Corporation,[2] an immensely insightful management book, diagrams the contrasting internal dynamics of trust-based and control-based organizations.

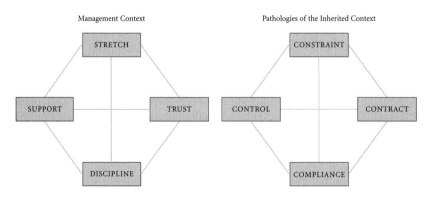

Love centered/Trust based   Fear centered/Control based

From *The Individualized Corporation* by Christopher A. Bartlett and Sumantra Ghoshal © 1997 by Christopher Bartlett and Sumantra Ghoshal (pp. 146, 153). Reprinted by permission of HarperCollins Publishers.

Let this sink in: *Organizations centered on fear do not trust the people they are leading.*

The result of this trust deficit? Leadership is compelled to create a contractual relationship with employees based on firm control and ongoing compliance. In this climate, the employee's relationship to the organization rests on three morale-draining and growth-busting foundations: *contract, control, and constraint.*

What a difference from love-centered organizations based upon trust! Relying upon the self-discipline of the individual, trusting leaders create trusting relationships with accountability. Employees receive the support they need to accomplish the goals of their positions and are thus challenged to stretch to their highest capacity. In this environment, the employee's relationship to the organization rests on three morale-boosting and growth-inducing foundations: *support, trust, and potential.*

Faced with such models, a leader's mind may swirl with large-scale questions. The internal monologue might be something along these lines: "I want to trust my people and delegate to them the appropriate authority. I also, in theory, want to give up some control in the organization I'm leading because I know that can only help us grow. However, because of past experience and gut intuition, I'm skeptical. *How do I relinquish control without losing it totally—or even creating chaos around here?*"

I'll try to answer that question in step-by-step fashion through-out the rest of this chapter. To begin, let's return to our analogy, through which we can imagine the equivalent results of certain organizational actions as if they occurred in a human body. For example, when *fear* rules a person's inner life over the long term—creating accompanying reactive *control* mechanisms—psychologists call it OCD (obsessive-compulsive disorder). Fear creates the obsessions; compulsive rituals attempt to relieve the fear. Here's what manifests when illness-inducing fear dominates a person's internal landscape:

- *Hoarding*—a terrifying reluctance to throw or give things away, regardless of value or usefulness;

- *Perfectionism*—an intense aversion to saying something wrong, leaving out details, making mistakes, taking risks, or letting things be less than ideal;

- *Checking and Counting*—obsessively going over and over, and/or repeatedly checking and counting, ordinary matters about a process or other elements in the immediate surroundings;

- *Slowness and Repetition*—methodically functioning with excruciating deliberateness, doing everything in repeatable ways to alleviate the terror of being mistaken or the shame of being in error.[3]

Most organizations and churches would never consider themselves either obsessive or compulsive, yet OCD-like traits do characterize many of their leaders and systems. Those that stay or become healthy—or at least choose to become healthier—give concrete instances of what happens when people are valued and treated with respect.

For example, one church asked me to help "re-create their climate," and, specifically, its leaders wanted structure and processes based on increased trust. I shared with them one of the implications of having a trust-based organization: *volunteers receive genuine authority*—and they notice the difference!

Months later, one volunteer contrasted her experience with this new structure against her experience under the "old way we used to do things around here": "When I used to volunteer, the staff person would tell me exactly what he wanted done. Then I'd just go ahead and do it. Volunteering was so . . . *booorrring!*" In addition, she usually felt underappreciated and overlooked. Now, with the trust-based approach, she's a vital part of the visioning and decision-making processes within her ministry team. "I'm excited and motivated," she says. "I finally get a say in where we're going and how we're getting there. It's like night and day for me!"

A good friend, "Kathy," was a volunteer intern in her church before deciding to take a job in another state. After relocating, she immediately got involved in a local church there; six months after that, she called. "I can't believe how much energy it takes to get anything accomplished!" she lamented.

She'd considered it in depth, investing heavily in comparing her experiences in the two churches, and here's what she concluded: "Dave, in permission-giving structures where trust is involved, the amount of time for a good idea to become reality is about three weeks. In my current church, a permission-hindering organization with all the control at the center, I estimate about three *years* to accomplish the same thing!"

Honestly: Why wouldn't we desire to work within permission-giving organizations? *The Individualized Corporation*[4] lays out a step-by-step process for creating this type of structure, as diagrammed here:

Management Context and Individual Behavior

From *The Individualized Corporation* by Christopher A. Bartlett and Sumantra Ghoshal © 1977 by Christopher Bartlett and Sumantra Ghoshal (p. 173). Reprinted by permission of HarperCollins Publishers.

Now let's begin applying this process to the concept of *building an organization around trust and accountability*. (In the next chapter we'll expand the discussion into how such an organization looks at the system-and-structure level.) A summary:

(1) Embed a sense of self-discipline.
(2) Provide a supportive environment.
(3) Create a trust-based culture.

Each of these "legs" of a permission-giving organization also has three related tasks that help accomplish the step; I'll define and describe each.

STEP #1: EMBED SELF-DISCIPLINE

How can you tell you're in a self-disciplined group? It usually comes through in easily recognizable positive behaviors. If you're the leader, you find people communicating back to you in timely ways, cheerfully following through on assignments. If you're a staff member or volunteer, you have a sense of taking responsibility for your own schedule and actions, thus avoiding excuses or blame-shifting. Three sub-steps help create organizational self-discipline:

(A) Establish clear standards and expectations.
(B) Provide equal access to important information.
(C) Create a constructive peer-review process.

Since the things we're talking about are the very things most people actually *want*, here's how they might ask for them in their own words.

"OKAY, WHAT'S *REALLY* EXPECTED AROUND HERE?"

Yes, they want to know what's expected, what the standards are, and whether they're succeeding. Therefore, establish (and publicize far and wide) your clear standards and expectations. Otherwise, your people will make up their own.

How will you communicate these guidelines? Picture a leader addressing her organization. She might say: "We want you to have lots of autonomy and freedom. But that can only happen if all of us first have a clear picture of the parameters. Thereafter, you can be free to manage yourself, since we believe you are more than capable of living up to those standards."

"CAN I ACCESS WHAT I NEED TO KNOW?"

Once the standards are in place, people need open access to organizational information. For one thing, they need to see how goals and objectives are tracked. In church settings, for example, you can measure certain tangible targets on at least a yearly basis. (What was our attendance in February? How many people are currently in small groups?)

Permission-giving organizations know that those on the front lines of ministry must be in touch with such information. All members should be invited to know and work with it so they can make appropriate adjustments or brainstorm creative ways to tackle problems and respond to developing trends.

"SO, HOW AM I DOING, FOLKS?"

Let's say you're well on your way to embedding self-discipline. Now add a regular peer-review process that incorporates clearly stated benchmarks. People trust a review process when it comes from their peers; they also trust outside "industry" standards more than the ones self-generated by their superiors (because of possible political agendas). Find out what's working best in parallel organizations, and do some comparisons in your reviews.

An added benefit is that when peers give each other feedback they also tend to create natural, informal accountability. When a report comes out, either good or bad, peers often encourage one another to correct the problems—without employee-employer baggage getting in the way. The potential for fear and/or shaming is minimized, and the idea is, *We're in this together, so let's help each other succeed.*

STEP #2: PROVIDE A SUPPORTIVE ENVIRONMENT

After embedding an environment of self-discipline, the next step is to create a supportive climate in which self-regulation can flourish and grow. Once again, the management theory in *The Individualized Corporation* suggests three related tasks.

(A) *Create a framework of consistently loosening control.*
(B) *Develop a balance between disciplined implementation and openness to challenges of the process.*
(C) *Learn to accept failure.*

"CAN YOU LOOSEN UP A LITTLE, GUYS?"

As leaders gradually loosen control, they can transition to a supportive environment; however, the most common mistake is trying to get there too quickly. A big surprise to many church leaders, for example, is the reluctance of laypeople to take hold of authority and responsibility after years of passively bowing down before it. They have to be coached into this process, which often will involve patiently training them in vision-casting, decision-making, and working effectively in leadership teams. As management reins are progressively relaxed, people *become* ready to assume the responsibility of self-discipline. (It's interesting, by way of comparison, to study the transitions of nations under recently overthrown dictatorships. When they're invited to begin responding as free citizens, they may display a similar reluctance. They too must learn how to be responsible within the context of newfound freedom.)

"SUPPOSE I DON'T LIKE WHAT'S HAPPENING HERE?"

The healthy organization will balance disciplined implementation with a willingness to hear legitimate critique and then adjust accordingly. You see, as controls loosen and people gain a voice in process and direction, an important tension quickly arises. People with a voice may wish to change things!

Maybe some elements really have needed changing for a long time. All well and good. Make the change.

But here leaders must also help to maintain the balance between execution and challenge. If the challenges cause the organization to stop producing completely or to miss significant goals and targets, then the challenges need to be wisely prioritized or diligently planned over the long haul. Rome wasn't built in a day, and organizations don't change overnight.

Some situations dictate the challenges simply needing to be limited to "the ones that won't cause total chaos here." The important thing is that the voices of challenge are not silenced or swept under the rug; the whole team takes responsibility for continuing to meet organizational objectives.

In *most* scenarios, the real difficulty in opening up authority is not people's unwillingness to accept responsibility. It's not even the possibility that doing so will somehow derail general or overall goals. *The big challenge comes in getting the managers and leaders to surrender control.*

When I'm consulting, this is one question they commonly ask of me: "How am I to act differently as a manager of this area of ministry (or work)?" I try to help them grasp the difference between control-oriented management and coaching-based relationship. I encourage them to switch their approach from "telling statements" to "offering questions." With those they're supervising, these leaders have been accustomed to telling: "This is what I want you to do." Conversely, suppose an employee or volunteer approaches with a significant problem. The leader can ask:

- In your view, what is the cause of the problem?

- What are you and your team going to do to fix it?

- How can I help?

Through these inquiries, the manager isn't taking the control back on herself. She's allowing the team to solve the problem with her help where it's welcome.

"I BLEW IT THIS TIME, OKAY?"

Okay. What did you learn? And how could you do it differently—better, more effectively, more productively—next time?

People will make mistakes, and within appropriate boundaries, you want to endorse this. Failure can start a process toward future improvement; in fact, such improvements may never have come about *without* the initial failure. Though failure itself isn't a good thing, it can actualize good consequences. An organization can be ready to capitalize by becoming more understanding of (and realistic about) failure in its people.

Once the controls are removed and a new relationship blossoms between supervisors and their people, folks will feel empowered to take risks and challenge the way things are done. If they're not making any mistakes, chances are they aren't risking creativity or stretching beyond their comfort zones. The 3M Company in St. Paul, Minnesota, legendary for encouraging such stretching, has a cannon on their campus. When someone makes a really wondrous mistake, they shoot off that big gun. Hey, if you're going to risk great success (and therefore risk a possible embarrassing failure), then go ahead and do it with a *bang*! Many fantastic 3M products have come into being because someone experimented a little . . . and suffered through a few cannon blasts.

STEP #3: CREATE A TRUST-BASED CULTURE

As you continue embedding a culture of self-discipline and continue to set up supportive structures for freedom and creativity, you can take the third step (and sub-steps) toward becoming a permission-giving organization: Create a culture of trust.

(A) Grow in transparency and openness.
(B) Pursue fairness and equity in management decisions.
(C) Live by a shared set of core values.

"MAY I SEE THE REAL YOU, PLEASE?"

Trust within organizations bases itself on not hiding things from employees, on allowing transparency and openness to permeate the entire environment. Top leaders do not hold all the information cards, using them to control and manipulate others into doing what they want. They see their role as being framers for organizational issues that are then opened up through the process for those in other roles to help solve them.

Over and over again, when I have set before ministry teams the challenges they face, they get excited and engaged—*when they're allowed to figure out for themselves the way to proceed.* This dynamic can occur in any group where transparent and open leaders allow others to see their strengths and weaknesses, their hopes and dreams, their flaws and foibles. These leaders are willing to let others exercise their gifts in direction-setting and problem-solving. They aren't threatened by those who are "merely human," because they've freely revealed themselves as fully human too.

"HOW ABOUT PLAYING BY THE RULES?"

People will quickly close down and not share openly if they detect unfairness in their managers. Since clear expectations have been established, with open access to information, management must not proceed to ignore these agreements and treat others unfairly.

I once witnessed a vote taken while a key staff member was on vacation—a vote that had substantial impact on this person's future. The church was running out of space, and some portion of the overall programming needed to be moved off the main campus to a nearby school.

Guess whose ministry was moved?

The rest of the staff voted to take the vacationer's ministry out of town and down the street for two years—without even waiting for input. What happens in the wake of such behavior? An immediate breaking of trust. And broken trust takes twice as long to repair (if ever) as it takes to establish.

"COULD WE AT LEAST SHARE THE VALUES?"

Finally, trust is reinforced not primarily by vision but by a shared set of values. People agree to follow these together, holding each other accountable along the way. To paraphrase Ghoshal and Bartlett in *The Individualized Corporation*:

> *People are loyal not to a particular boss or company so much as the values they believe in and find satisfying. Shared values lead to a collective identity, a sense of unity and solidarity that facilitates trusting and sharing and thereby supports the horizontal flows that are so vital to an organization.*[5]

Remember, an organization does not *create* values, but discovers and clarifies values that are already embedded in its people. This discovery isn't easy; it involves discerning the emotional and intuitive responses within and among members. The question *What do we really stand for around here?* can't be answered merely with logic and analysis. Even so, the hard work of value discovery is worth it—shared values unify and motivate everyone like nothing else can.

GO AHEAD—*BELIEVE* IN THESE PEOPLE!

When the three important legs of a permission-giving organization stand solidly in place, trust and accountability become the norm within a group; control and compliance become the exception, not the rule. Interdependency flows among the various people and departments, and the word *synergy* begins to have real meaning—the whole being much larger than the sum of its parts. For me, the image that best reflects this reality is the body of Christ: a mutually supportive, synergistic, networked, and interlinked organizational structure. (That's the theme of chapter 4.)

Before we proceed, however, let me clearly restate our theme: *Leaders must cultivate a fundamental belief in the people they are leading.* If they don't, they won't want to give away any control or authority, and without such release, an organization will eventually dry up.

> *True empowerment occurs only when it grows out of a reciprocal system of faith. Those deep in the organization must have faith in their company and its leadership, and senior management must have faith in the people in its organization. Working together, it is this mutually supportive system that allows the individual organization members to have faith in themselves, which in turn provides the engine for entrepreneurial initiative that drives the corporate engine.[6]*

To put this within a theological framework, over against human sin and brokenness, leadership must believe Ephesians 3:20–21 deep within their souls:

> *Now to him who is able to do immeasurably more than all we ask or imagine, according to his power that is at work within us, to him be glory in the church and in Christ Jesus throughout all generations, for ever and ever! Amen.*

Do you believe God is working in your people like this? If so, trust Him to be successful.

FOR REFLECTION

Use this space to write down your reflections, reactions, insights, and responses to this chapter and its central question.

Do I believe in the people I'm leading?

FOUR

What Is Your Definition of Success?

I began my ministerial career in memorable fashion. The church was medium-sized, averaging five hundred worshipers in two services. I was on staff, heading up several ministries for youth and adults. And I was truly enjoying it. But then, after just three years, the bottom dropped out. We went from four pastors to one pastor in a nine-month stretch.

I was that one pastor.

Lord, how is this possible? How am I going to do all this work?

I bit the bullet, tightened the bootstraps, put my nose to the grindstone . . . (I think you get the idea: I worked really hard). Soon I was managing four different job descriptions, and I kept at it over the next two years before a new senior pastor finally entered the scene.

Saying I was pleased by this long-needed addition would be colossally understated. I was *ecstatic.* I was also shell-shocked, so overly fatigued that I didn't sleep for three straight nights after the installation service.

As I lay awake, too exhausted for slumber, it dawned on me that maybe this is not God's idea of ministry. *Isn't something missing here?* I wondered.

THE MISSING INGREDIENT

The answer, of course, was a resounding *yes!* Much was missing in my go-it-alone approach. As a young pastor, I had lots to learn.

Over the past decade, many have written about permission-giving structures and cultures of trust. Not everyone is happy to embrace these models. The standard critique goes something like this:

"Look, David, even developing trust-based, supportive, permission-giving structures doesn't automatically create excited, motivated, and successful people. In fact, I know by experience that it can lead to people doing a lot of things the organization doesn't want done! Or it can lead to waiting for something that never takes place because the people aren't ready to take advantage of this wonderful environment. Especially in volunteer settings, people have many other priorities in their lives. They don't naturally put 'ministry' at the top of their priorities in any given year."

Nice try. But here's where the missing ingredient comes in to save the day: It's *equipping,* a most excellent biblical concept. People need to be equipped in preparation to take on their own ministries. If the structures and cultures are dysfunction-free, and if people are equipped to serve in that healthy environment, successful ministry can follow.

In fact, a few years ago Leadership Network did a related survey, coming to the conclusion that only 12 percent of those who have identified their gifts and talents will actually engage them in church life—*unless they have some type of mentoring.* Mentoring might be informal; it might come through regular involvement in a small group; it may come from serving with a ministry team. *However* it occurs, equipping is essential, which leads us to a passage filled with leadership "job descriptions."

He . . . gave some to be apostles, some to be prophets, some to be evangelists, and some to be pastors and teachers, to prepare God's people for works of service, so that the body of Christ may be built up until we all reach unity in the faith and in the knowledge of the Son of God and become mature, attaining to the whole measure of the fullness of Christ.

Then we will no longer be infants, tossed back and forth by the waves, and blown here and there by every wind of teaching and by the cunning and craftiness of men in their deceitful scheming. Instead, speaking the truth in love, we will in all things grow up into him who is the Head, that is, Christ. From him the whole body, joined and held together by every support- ing ligament, grows and builds itself up in love, as each part does its work.

EPHESIANS 4:11–16

Notice the process. Paul begins by pointing to certain spiritual gifts, exercised by the various kinds of church leaders, who are to prepare God's people for works of service. After they *prepare* the people, the people are able to *perform* their ministries, and the body of Christ grows into maturity. A mature Christian fellowship won't fall prey to the ravages of false teaching, but instead will grow deeper in love with, and closer to, its Head.

When they truly understand this passage, pastors and layleaders tend to shift their definition of successful church work. This defi- nition once rested upon a personal-development vision: "How do I build a successful ministry for myself, using and developing my gifts and talents to serve the body of Christ?" A fine sentiment, but hardly the biblical model. When we integrate Paul's teaching, our definition of success changes radically: "How many people have I thoroughly prepared for their ministries so they can serve the body of Christ?"

EQUIPPING AS SUCCEEDING

This shift produces dramatic results. Remember my "sleepless in the saddle" story? I decided then and there to focus on equipping people rather than trying to be the Lone Ranger minister in all things at all times. I thought of the ancient desert fathers (a protest movement against worldliness in the early church) who spoke of busyness as "moral laziness."

> *Busyness can also be an addictive drug, which is why its victims are increasingly referred to as "workaholics." Busyness acts to repress our inner fears and personal anxieties, as we scramble to achieve an enviable image to display to others. We become "outward" people, obsessed with how we appear, rather than "inward" people, reflecting on the meaning of our lives.*[1]

Does this mean I could be so overwhelmingly busy that I lose the meaning of true ministry? Yes, I could, if I failed to equip the flock entrusted to my care. Clearly, according to the Scriptures, equipping is my essential purpose.

So in my second church, one with three thousand members, I spent most of my time preparing and equipping layleaders to minister. This ministry was ten times the size of my first, but I wasn't exhausted—I felt energized by everything God was doing through the empowered laypeople around me. Many others could tell a similar story.

In a wonderful book titled *Liberating the Laity*, R. Paul Stevens points out that our educational system ties "professionalism" around ministry that sets leaders up for a false definition of success. He lists these mitigating factors:

(1) *They have full-time work with full financial support.*
(2) *They have a quasi-unique function that has some social significance.*
(3) *They move toward increasing specialization.*
(4) *They work in an environment that discourages "amateurism," the assumption being that one well-trained person can do it better.*[2]

Thus pastors misunderstand their role. And even when they (and their layleaders) *do* choose to operate within an equipping approach, they must concurrently work hard at changing the congregation's mentality.

Wayne Cordero, pastor of a large church in Hawaii, challenges the thinking of laypeople around the country. He begins by asking a large audience how many present are full-time ministers. When I heard him speak, I was sitting in a crowd of four thousand people; about four hundred of us raised our hands.

Wayne said, "Thank you." Then he told us what he believes God is up to: "God wants to take a full-time minister and disguise her as a chemical engineer, so we can win the chemical engineers to Christ. . . . He wants to take a full-time minister and disguise him as the elementary principal, so we can influence the character and values of countless students. . . . He wants to take a full-time minister and disguise her as a stay-at-home mom, so we can build the children for the church's next generation."

Though his point became obvious after the first couple of examples, Wayne went on this way for ten minutes. He then paused and asked, "How many full-time ministers do we have with us today?" Four thousand hands shot up.

"That is the church of Jesus Christ," he concluded. "That is our definition of success."

Let's go back to the human body and consider a potential serious imbalance. Several weeks ago while taking private Pilates sessions to build my exercise regimen, I learned something about how my body had been functioning over the years. It seems my larger muscle groups—my strong thigh muscles, for example—had been compensating for what many smaller back and abdominal groups should have been doing.

It made sense; for one thing, I was an avid skier and soccer player. Problem was, many muscles were simply along for the ride while my legs did most of the labor. I had to work hard to find and get in touch with some of them—they were weak and underdeveloped, having hidden behind the big players, my dominant celebrity muscles.

Despite the challenge, the transformation has been wonderful. As I've helped my thighs learn to do less and relax, the other groups have begun to strengthen, and they too are engaged in promoting my overall physical health. I now realize that if I'd continued with this imbalance, I'd likely have experienced an unnecessary future injury.

That is, I was moving gradually toward a crisis point at which my weaknesses would become evident, and I'd likely suffer a strain, a sprain, or maybe even a broken bone. Serious weight lifters stress exercising *complementary* muscle groups equally; for example, having strong biceps and weak triceps is a setup for injury.

A similar phenomenon shows up in church systems. When the minister's role leans toward *dominant,* the significant roles of others tend to go *dormant.* Could he pull back a bit? Could he learn to trust the strengths and abilities of the body's other "muscles"? Perhaps he suffers from a fear that "ordinary folks" just can't do the job; yet if he's willing to face and overcome his trepidation and let the other muscles contribute, he often finds them to be even more competent in many ways than himself.

In any case, we do know that not every leader has every strength. Some laypeople will do certain things better than their full-time pastor. If nothing else, it makes sense on a purely practical level to shift to an equipping ministry.

MAKING THE ALL-IMPORTANT SHIFT

Maybe you're saying, "David, I agree with the theology here, and I accept the management principles you're advocating. But this is difficult! It is *not* easy to shift to equipping as my vision of success."

I feel your pain. All of us who undertake this adjustment must face some emotional, gut-wrenching changes—within ourselves and within our ministry structures. After all, we want to be useful and competent in our chosen vocations . . . and *we want to be seen that way by others*. Productivity, impact, significance, and fulfillment are important words for us; in shifting to equipping, we fear the loss of competence, influence, usefulness, completion. As irrational as it sounds when we say it aloud, a voice inside us whispers, "What will *I* do if I prepare everybody *else* to minister?"

Let me encourage you. I've experienced both sides of this equation. First, I've found that watching thousands of people fulfilling their ministries dwarfs the impact of seeing my own development. Second, in the process of doing all the equipping, there are plenty of opportunities to use my gifts and talents in significant ways. Be assured, I always have plenty to do.

Consider one of my case studies of two ministers. Both started their journeys in the sixties, both led successful ministries in the seventies and eighties, and both passed the baton to others in the nineties. Their stories illustrate the difference an equipping shift can make.

The first man saw himself primarily as a minister of the gospel. Physically, he was what I can only describe as majestic—people were naturally drawn to him and his elegant self-presentation. He became the hottest ticket in town, known especially for his dynamic preaching. To this day, whenever people talk about that church, his name automatically comes to their lips as they fondly recall his pulpit presence.

I came to know about this church in the nineties, having been invited to consult with its leadership on a number of topics. They'd fallen on hard times; together, we needed to explore in order to find out why. Here's what we eventually concluded: (1) This wonderful minister would not let go, and (2) there had been very little equipping of leaders around him.

Simple truths. Devastating impact.

When laypeople had to voice their disapproval of his leadership style and decisions, many simply left the church, while others hung on until he left the ministry. A new senior minister finally took over, but that relationship was quickly terminated as the church continued downhill. Former staff members are still serving in other congregations; their senior pastor had so tightly clutched his unfortunate definition of success that their ministries weren't going to happen at his church. To this date, they continue to struggle, no longer mentioned much around the city.

Now consider the second man. He too was highly gifted. When I met him during the eighties while doing research on thriving churches, his church came up over and over. Everyone hailed it as an example of ministry done well.

When I repeatedly asked, "Who is the senior pastor there?" nobody seemed to have any idea! In fact, I knew the names of multiple associate pastors and layleaders long before I discovered this man's name. When he retired, one associate pastor became the executive pastor, and the church charged ahead, stronger than ever. A well-known preacher later took over the senior pastorate, and this church is becoming one of the most outstanding in its area.

I realize that many, many factors influence churches in stories like these. However, I'm convinced of the profound impact of *altered definitions of success*. One pastor saw as his goal the development of his own ministry, the other saw himself as an equipper of many ministries. One church died with the leaving of its leader, the other grew stronger as its leader trained others to thrive.

What exactly is the equipping task of pastors and layleaders? R. Paul Stevens suggests that the apostle's Greek word in Ephesians for "equip," *katartismon,* has six rich images standing behind it that can help us nail down the nature of equipping in our churches today.[3]

(1) SET THE BONE

In ancient times, doctors would "equip" a bone that was out of joint by bringing it back into right alignment with the whole body; unless this happens, the body will never be fully healed and functional. The same is true for the body of Christ: People must be brought into relationship with a few others with whom they can build close relationships. They align themselves by learning to walk through life together; if they do not, they will never substantially develop as Christians. Therefore, this is my first question in working with those I'm seeking to equip: "Are you in a small group?" People must feel they belong before they begin to develop as ministers.

(2) MEND THE NETS

Ancient fisherman "equipped" their broken nets. People who experience brokenness (and we all do) need mending—support and encouragement from Christian brothers and sisters, including church leaders. Deep levels of brokenness may require creating a special atmosphere for mending. Big soul hurts or heart rips can't be shuffled aside—until they're addressed, other endeavors toward spiritual development do little long-term good. The suffering person must be healed and restored, to some degree, in order to grow.

(3) MOLD THE CLAY

For many, the third image becomes the next important step after being relationally connected to the body. Picture a potter "equipping" a pot by centering it on the wheel, molding it with his hands, and fashioning it into the shape he envisioned. Christians, too, need formation, which comes by way of an ongoing life of worship and of devotion, centered in Christ through the Holy Spirit. Thereby, through God's grace, we become the person He intends, growing more and more into the likeness of His Son. We cannot grow without this experiential touch of God's gentle hand. It's part of the ongoing preparation for ministering and serving in congregations and organizations.

(4) TEACH THE STUDENT

This fourth image has a much greater impact on a person if the first three aspects of equipping are already in place. A teacher "equips" her students by giving them the information and skills they need to do their work. Biblical and theological input begins to form their minds; they obtain God's kingdom perspective, and they implement a Christian worldview as His Word transforms their character, values, and relationships:

> *All Scripture is God-breathed and is useful for teaching, rebuk-ing, correcting and training in righteousness, so that the man of God may be thoroughly equipped for every good work.*
> 2 TIMOTHY 3:16–17

Many of us are familiar with the teaching, rebuking, and correcting power of the Word in our lives. But look again at the second half of this text: "training in righteousness." Knowing the Scriptures is part of being equipped; an equipper-teacher prepares people for their good works.

(5) ASSIGN THE TASKS

A builder in ancient times "equipped" a project by placing people in the right jobs and assignments. Today this involves iden-tifying church members' gifts, talents, and passions. *Then* they can invest in the right work, both within congregations and in the world at large. While they begin at this point to minister to others, they're still being equipped on an ongoing basis.

(6) REPLACE THAT STONE

A mason must be ready to replace any stones that might fall out of a wall. We can apply this to our need to plan ahead for the inev-itable—volunteers will leave town, choose not to sign up again, go into the hospital, or (you name it). Another solid reason to practice ongoing equipping over time: New leadership will then be available to step in as needed.

Paul probably didn't have all six of these images in mind when he wrote his letter to Ephesus. Nevertheless, they can help us remember the different ways in which Christian leaders release pre-pared people into ministry. That is the overarching idea behind them all: *Laypeople need preparation in order to be fully released into the ministries they are called to do.*

Now, to spread the ministry work this way, leaders must create systems where people with certain gifts and talents can be equipped to carry out their calling. Such systems might look like this:

(1) The nurturing system *helps people connect and form relationships in the church. Gifts and/or talents: hospitality, evangelism, shepherding.*

(2) The care system *encourages and supports through offering counseling resources, support groups, classes, retreats. Gifts and/or talents: healing, mercy, encouragement, counseling, as well as natural talents, such as listening, empathy, etc.*

(3) The celebration system *helps people center on God and be nourished by the Holy Spirit on an ongoing basis. Gifts and/or talents: preaching, intercession, artistic natural talents, such as music, art, writing, etc.*

(4) The learning system *conveys principles of Scripture and other sources of knowledge through myriad effective methods. Gifts and/or talents: teaching, prophecy, knowledge, wisdom.*

(5) The transforming system *creates atmospheres where people can be changed into disciples that reflect God's agendas in their lives. Gifts and talents are teaching, prophecy, intercessory prayer, and shepherding.*

(6) The equipping system: *All the above are equipping, but this is the formal system that helps people discover their giftedness and then trains them to begin ministering inside and outside the church. Gifts and/or talents: leadership, discernment, administration.*

Churches that are serious about equipping and preparing people usually have such systems in full operation. They look and feel different from place to place, but they all have the same goal— to equip the saints for the work of the ministry. When these various systems are in place, we can trace the typical journey of an involved layperson. Mr. Jones starts by attending a church, then he

- forms relationships with a few others in a smaller group;

- begins feeling, "I *belong* here";

- engages in special supportive atmospheres for mending and heal-ing;

- becomes ready to learn and grow through instruction;

- takes on the worldview of the kingdom;

- gradually adjusts his priorities toward ministry and service;

- identifies his gifts and passions;

- seeks specific training and preparation for a particular form of service within and beyond the congregation.

Isn't this a wonderful progression? Would you enjoy watching this happen, over and over again? Would helping it happen feel like a rewarding ministry?

Leaders of these kinds of churches have a clear vision of success. Their overarching goal is to *increase the number of people who go through this process,* to deeper and deeper levels, to greater and greater degrees. As more and more are released into ministry, they consider themselves all the more successful. Pastors and leaders of these churches always have three things on their minds when establishing any of the above processes:

- What is the goal of this process in our church (for example, the care system)?

- Who can I work with in forming the ministry team to oversee the development of this process?

- What type of training, coaching, and resources do volunteers/ staff need to get this team functioning—and, in turn, what type of training, coaching, and resources will *they* offer to *their* volunteers to keep this process effective and improving?

Often in order to emphasize the importance of this shift in thinking, I will say to them: "I'm not going to ask how your ministry is going. I want to ask instead a more important question: *How is your equippery going?*" (I'm asking, of course, about how many people they're equipping for ministry.) This approach should come as no surprise to us, for we see it playing out in the life of Jesus, whom some see as the world's greatest CEO.

> *In only three years Christ defined a mission and formed strategies to carry it out. With a staff of twelve unlikely men, He organized Christianity, which today has branches in all the world's countries and a 32.4 percent share of the world's population—twice as big as its nearest rival. Managers want to develop people to their full potential, taking ordinary people and making them extraordinary. This is what Christ did with His disciples. Jesus was the most effective executive in history. The results He achieved are second to none.*[4]

Churches implementing these systems begin making an enormous impact upon the believers and the communities around them. They make a difference in everything they touch.

An equipping ministry stands or falls upon its quality of leadership, especially upon its leaders' definitions of success. So as we close, I raise the question once again: "What is your definition of success, based on the track record you see so far?"

FOR REFLECTION

Use this space to write down your reflections, reactions, insights, and responses to this chapter and its central question.

What is my definition of success?

FIVE

Where Is Your Focus?

You've seen it happen, maybe even to you. That funny jig people do when they suddenly face multiple options and must decide . . . *now*. Maybe you've stood in the lobby of a large building, facing a bank of elevators. You push the Up button . . . all five doors open at once . . . and the embarrassing little dance begins. You hope no one's watching as you attempt to regain composure, overcome your split-second paralysis, and choose one.

This reminds me of something I hear regularly from leaders: "There are so many things I could be doing, so many directions to take, theories to know, people to meet, and books to read. I mean, I'm hopping back and forth, one foot to the other. I busy myself with countless daily tasks. As a leader, where should I *really* focus my attention?"

Obviously, I'm convinced we need to answer this question. In equipping people to prepare and placing them for service within a ministry, we can default to the elevator dance if we're not careful, if we don't learn to focus our attention. To understand the importance, take a look at two visual puzzles.

In this optical illusion, no actual lines form the two white triangles. Yet those triangles dominate your vision; the various individual pie-cut circles work together to form a bigger picture.[1]

In the next one, it's more difficult to visualize the "whole" that the parts are forming:[2]

What do you see? Some people immediately notice a male jazz musician playing a saxophone in profile. Others see a beautiful woman's face. My point regarding both pictures: What you see depends on your focus. It's the difference between zeroing in on the parts or pulling back and gazing on the whole.

This difference has profound application to our leadership approach. It's truly a matter of growth or decline, success or failure as your ministry seeks to grow. Why? Because *leaders must learn to focus on the whole work rather than on individuals doing it.*

WHERE ARE YOU LOOKING?

Leaders must primarily focus on how individuals work *together* to form the whole of the ministry. Yes, we care deeply about individuals. Yes, we love them and relate to them warmly. We make friends and grow strong bonds of fellowship at many levels. But our vision for the ministry always takes in the whole and centers there.

Before we look at the specifics of how this works in organizations, let's begin with Paul's teaching in 1 Corinthians about the body of Christ. The text is long, so please also read its entirety in your Bible. I'll quote parts of it here:

There are different kinds of gifts, but the same Spirit. There are different kinds of service, but the same Lord. There are different kinds of working, but the same God works all of them in all men.

Now to each one the manifestation of the Spirit is given for the common good. . . .

The body is a unit, though it is made up of many parts; and though all its parts are many, they form one body. So it is with Christ. . . .

God has combined the members of the body and has given greater honor to the parts that lacked it, so that there should be no division in the body, but that its parts should have equal concern for each other. If one part suffers, every part suffers with it; if one part is honored, every part rejoices with it.

Now you are the body of Christ, and each one of you is a part of it. . . .

Are all apostles? Are all prophets? Are all teachers? Do all work miracles? Do all have gifts of healing? Do all speak in tongues? Do all interpret? But eagerly desire the greater gifts.

And now I will show you the most excellent way.

If I speak in the tongues of men and of angels, but have not love, I am only a resounding gong or a clanging cymbal. If I have the gift of prophecy and can fathom all mysteries and all knowledge, and if I have a faith that can move mountains, but have not love, I am nothing. If I give all I possess to the poor and surrender my body to the flames, but have not love, I gain nothing.

12:4–7, 12, 24–27, 29–31; 13:1–3

The Corinthian church members are people in conflict. They've divided into factions. Some are feeling left out and insignificant; others believe they don't need certain less-important members to keep the church going. Naturally, all of this distresses Paul. He writes for many reasons and covers many topics, but fundamentally he endeavors to compel everyone to focus not on individual differences and conflicts but on the whole church. He wants them to see that *everyone* plays a unique role in ministry and community. For our purposes here, notice three main themes in this passage:

(1) We are one body,
(2) with specialization, but
(3) with no division.

First, Paul emphasizes that the Spirit has designed the body as it is. The church doesn't rest upon the merits or choices of any one individual or group of individuals:

(1) The gifts, service, and workings are different in individual people, but God works in all of them.
(2) The various manifestations were given by the Spirit as He determined, not by any effort from anyone.
(3) We are one body, by baptism and by drinking of one Spirit.

Second, the apostle points to the body's differentiation into separate parts. Why is this necessary? Because it needs specialization if it is to be fully functional in accomplishing its mission to be the embodiment of Jesus on earth until He comes again. We must be His witnesses—the hands and feet, the heart and mouth of our

Lord—until that blessed Day. Again, Paul fleshes this out:

(1) *The body is a unit, made up of many parts yet forming one body.*
(2) *God has arranged these various parts just as He wanted.*
(3) *If we did not have many different parts, we would not be a full human body.*

Third, Paul drives home the body's purpose: to have equal regard for one another, without division, and to operate at full capacity in ministry. He offers these supporting statements:

(1) *Differentiation is given for the common good, not for one individual to outshine the others.*
(2) *Special parts of the body cannot either opt out (feeling inferior) or push out other parts (thinking the others aren't needed).*
(3) *The result is indivisibility, equal regard, and fully functional ministry with focus on the body as a whole rather than individual or separate parts.*

Most Western Christian leaders know this Corinthians passage well, but they often miss its crucial implications for leadership. After all, our culture stresses *individual* performance and excellence, and it's hard for us to adjust our focus to the big picture when we persist in locking our eyes on the individual. The "army of one" mentality has burrowed deeply into our psyches.

RAMBO . . . OR AN ARMY OF MANY?

When years ago we took our little kids to Disney World, we spent some time at Epcot Center. At Epcot you can walk through the pavilions of several representative nations to "get into their world." You can eat that culture's food, hear its music, watch video presentations about its people, and buy its souvenirs.

I was especially taken with our own American pavilion, with all its beautiful photography and moving music about this magnificent country. As I walked into the main auditorium, however, something unusual caught my eye: statues of "The Spirits of America." On one side of the room sat the Spirit of Self-Reliance, embodied in a Native American chief. On the other side loomed the Spirit of Individualism, sculptured as a pioneering frontiersman. Standing near them was the Spirit of Independence, represented by a cowboy. Each ornate image pointed to a single permeating idea: the power of the individual.

This idea has long been counterbalanced in the United States with the Judeo-Christian sense of community. In *Habits of the Heart,* American sociologist and educator Robert Bellah called for a return to this heritage, warning that unchecked individualism was spinning out of control, and community—a focus on the whole— needed to be reemphasized in American culture.

His theme, of course, continues to be relevant today in our cult-of-personality society. We have our Superman, our Rambo, and our Spiderman. We have celebrity personas constantly pushing into the spotlight. We love to focus on their successes and failures, their foibles and peccadilloes. Even individuals we may "love to hate" keep our attention riveted to on-the-hour updates.

Where is our sense of community? Where is our recognition of its importance to society and to the health and growth of the church?

Eastern cultures, including the one of the New Testament, tend to focus much more on the community, paying attention to how individuals fit within the whole rather than honing in on individual performance. A marvelous example of this came to me from a Chinese-born Canadian at one of my conferences. We sat down to dinner in a cafeteria while discussing the differences between Western and Eastern cultures. "Do you have an everyday case in point?" I asked.

"Okay, start with how they're serving meals here," he replied. "In Western cultures, each person has an individual plate, which he fills up with all the food he'll be consuming; he sits down, individually, to eat. In Eastern cultures, we put plates in the center from which people continue to take small portions. It starts with the communal and then moves to the individual."

How does this have meaning for our leadership? I'd like to suggest: *We can do ministry more effectively in teams.* Even though this is fairly obvious after two decades of revolutionizing American business around team-based work, in many ways it's easy to forget. I've observed countless ministries still focusing heavily on individual performance and development.

For example, I watched two different sets of leaders run and develop the same ministry over a period of years. "Jim" led the first set. He was an entrepreneur with his own successful businesses and a dedicated volunteer leader at his church.

As Jim worked with one of the ministries, the senior pastor kept encouraging him to form a group around himself so he could share the workload. Jim attempted this once or twice, but his style was to *ask for help only when the load got too heavy.* The ministry grew to include over one hundred people, and over a period of five years Jim's burnout factor hit the stratosphere. He found it increasingly difficult to stay motivated, and when he began harboring bitterness and resentment, his pastor suggested a sabbatical.

Thankfully, Jim was followed by an energetic group looking for a big challenge. The pastor gladly put this ministry in their hands to shepherd over the next few years. And what a variety of skills and talent flourished! Musicians, administrators, teachers, accountants, broadcasters, social workers, mechanics—in less than six months they grew from a low of about twenty people (when Jim let go) to a high of more than five hundred.

Team meetings were actually fun, since they genuinely enjoyed each other's company. Three or four different people handled leadership responsibility over time, according to a rotating plan. Nobody wanted or needed to leave for burnout or lack of motivation. If someone asked a group member, "Who's leading this ministry?" he or she usually wouldn't name an individual—it just seemed more natural to say something about how "the whole team is shepherding it well."

CAN YOU LEAD WITH WHOLE-FOCUS SKILL?

During the seventies and eighties, a business-originated "team revolution" began working its way into the church. It hasn't been easy for many of us to adopt a totally different focus. Less dominant on our radars became the *individual* top performer; we've kept our eyes on top performing *teams* as well as on all that's needed to create them.

What *is* needed? While many niche books fill the shelves, one of my favorites is Glenn Parker's *Cross-Functional Teams.* In his introduction, he stresses the gargantuan mental shift:

> *A good concept is not enough [to be a successful business]; diversity is not enough [to be a successful business]. In practice, it requires a migration from a parochial view of the world—my function, my values, and my goals are paramount—to a broader view that says, we're all in this together. Success is team success, rewards are team rewards, and if the team fails, the members share the blame.*[3]

We'll be talking in detail about various aspects of team leadership in the next four chapters. For now, we also need to know the broad-based action steps and disciplines required for this change. I'd like to list the nine important dimensions of whole-focus leadership and describe each briefly.

WHOLE-FOCUS LEADERSHIP SETS GOALS TIED TO AUTHORITY AND DEFINED OUTCOMES

A team needs to know its *mission* and what *authority* it has to accomplish it. One of the related skills that leaders can learn is the ability to convey the big picture of both and then let the team do the work of defining specifics. Not only will a group-led process come up with more innovative ideas and directions than one individual can, but the team also will be energized and will experience a high level of ownership. After all, they themselves have generated their vision, goals, and objectives; the defined outcomes are of their own making, and because they've bought in at a profoundly personal level, they feel genuinely empowered. (The team's goals and defined outcomes can always be reviewed and modified by the organization's leadership, but the review usually becomes a mere formality.)

WHOLE-FOCUS LEADERSHIP GIVES TEAMS AUTHORITY WITH ACCOUNTABILITY

Empowering teams with the authority they need means developing an acceptance of risk and failure within limits. As a whole-focus leader, can you exercise this?

You'll alleviate some of your anxiety if you put together a solid training program and create a good accountability system. That way you can stay in touch with a team and work through problems as they occur. One of the great lessons of leadership is that *there are many tenable ways to reach the same outcomes.* Surrendering my way of doing it allows teams the unique expression of their personalities and talents. It's risky . . . and potentially exciting. *When empowering others, you must develop your own risk-tolerance.*

WHOLE-FOCUS LEADERSHIP CHOOSES/RECRUITS PEOPLE-GROUPS WITH DIVERSE SKILLS

Leaders tend to recruit just one person and then let him or her recruit the rest of the team. Sometimes this is most appropriate, but leaders within volunteer ministries often will be much more successful if they think in terms of *recruiting groups of people together.*

In this scenario, whole-focus leaders recognize that no single individual will bring to the table all the qualities required for success. An additional benefit of recruiting in groups is that many more people will say yes to a volunteer responsibility if they know the whole ministry won't depend upon them alone; they immediately see others joining them in shouldering the work.

WHOLE-FOCUS LEADERSHIP DESIGNS AND DELIVERS APPROPRIATE TEAM TRAINING

Effective churches offer some form of basic training for each area of ministry. This allows leaders to build common vision, basic skills, and knowledge among the teams. Team members also gain an awareness of the history and context of a ministry as they enter the processes utilized to carry out the work. Training allows "new" members to develop relationships with "old" members, and a continuity of leadership is established, over time, as ministries change and evolve.

WHOLE-FOCUS LEADERSHIP ALLOCATES RESOURCES AND GIVES ACCESS TO MORE

Teams *will* need a starting set of resources, but they also need ways of communicating the gradual development of their vision and the span of their influence. That is, they will likely need *more* resources! They must have a clearly defined way to ask for things, whether it is money, supplies, or personnel.

These requests must easily reach the appropriate leadership settings for timely consideration. Remember, when multiple ministries exist, a whole-focus leader's decisions about resources will influence the entire organization in certain directions. This is no small matter!

WHOLE-FOCUS LEADERSHIP REWARDS TEAM AND INDIVIDUAL SUCCESSES

Reward and recognition are planned into the flow of team processes. Especially in nonprofit circles, rewarding and recognizing people becomes essential to ongoing motivation. Whole-focus leaders stay on top of this, yet teams should also create systems for recognizing notable moments and milestones in the work, seeking a balance between rewarding group performance and individual contributions.

WHOLE-FOCUS LEADERSHIP MANAGES THE INTERFACE AMONG ALL TEAMS

Each team should know about the work being done by other teams. We're all in this together! Whole-focus leaders facilitate overall teamwork even as they help work out the appropriate boundaries among teams. Since these boundaries are constantly changing, wise leaders address them with win/win strategies that won't hinder the work at any level. They also protect a team when its specific work might be wasted or upstaged by other organizational agendas.

WHOLE-FOCUS LEADERSHIP UTILIZES A VARIETY OF GROUP-PROCESSING SKILLS

We'll talk more about this later, but two processes come to mind that especially apply to nonprofit settings. The first is called a "group covenant" (do your teams have one?), which is basic agreement about the group or team's interactions and activities, including vision, objectives, and goals. It includes how big they should be, how often and when they will meet, and which unique agreements will be established and observed among its members. For example, a team might have a confidentiality clause: "What's spoken in this group stays here." Simply put, whole-focus leaders help teams establish relational expectations and accomplishment standards *up front*.

A second helpful group process is to include more than one agenda in meetings. Especially in volunteer teams, people come together for more than the task at hand—they want to build relationships, grow as individuals (spiritually, socially, intellectually, vocationally), and contribute in significant ways. Therefore, meeting agendas should go beyond the most urgent item; for instance, consider relationship-building time, prayer time, study time, or other creative ways to meet a broader set of needs.

WHOLE-FOCUS LEADERSHIP ADJUSTS AND ADAPTS AS TEAMS EVOLVE AND CONDITIONS CHANGE

Simply put, such leaders must maintain ongoing willingness to adapt. Groups have seasons and life cycles, so leaders need flexibility—even *their* leadership styles will change over time. Whole-focus leaders never stop adjusting and adapting, changing and re-visioning. (Note: These are merely the nine basics of whole-focus team leadership. You can more deeply delve into these points in my small-group series called *People Together,* published by Faith Alive Press.)

Before we continue examining Christ-based leadership, once again I want to leave with you a key question: What is your focus? Are you zeroing in on a few top performers? If so, can you refocus your sights on excellent and dynamic ministry teams? Such groups can work corporately—as a body—to accomplish far more than any one individual. We just have to *see* it that way.

FOR REFLECTION

Use this space to write down your reflections, reactions, insights, and responses to this chapter and its central question.

Where is my focus?

SIX

Do You Have a Culture of Excellence or a Culture of Winning?

The crack of the bat, the swish of the net, the feel of leather and liniment. I loved it all as I grew up, competing on athletic fields of battle from my earliest days. As far as I was concerned (to misquote Robert Duvall), "There was nothing like the smell of sweat socks in the morning." Maybe that's why we (my buddies and I) spent all our free time in some kind of sport. Whether it called for racquets, clubs, or something strapped to our feet or bodies, one way or another we were going to compete.

Do you have a competitive spirit? If so, you may also be aware of a crucial distinction many athletes realize along the way: the difference between playing to be excellent and playing simply to beat the other guy.

Let me illustrate with tennis, one of my favorites. As a youngster I spent countless hours building my ground strokes, working on my serve and net game, adding various specialty shots along the way. Once I reached high school, however, my focus moved from *my* tennis game to the tennis *team.*

It was a subtle shift that made all the difference. As a squad, would we keep building on our excellent skills, or would we merely prepare to defeat our next opponent? Choosing the latter, here's what dominated my thinking: Match strategy, game plans, tactics that could psyche out an opposing player. It worked! I remember winning lots of matches against those with better fundamental skills; I'd just formed a more strategic approach to competition.

In competitive sports, as the name implies, a big part of the goal is to win. Never forget, though, that you can genuinely stop improving if you maintain a dogged and primary pursuit of first place.

WHEN GOOD TEAMS GO BAD

Do you ever read those sometimes unfortunate headlines in your sports section? They often appear on the morning after "Friday night lights," and parochial schools can lend particularly dramatic imagination to a gridiron contest: "Mary Queen of Angels Trounces Father Lopez" or "Holy Cross Pounds the Saints." Something just doesn't seem right . . .

It's one thing to stress winning in the sports world; it's another to carry this focus into our kingdom organizations. Here we're obviously *not* trying to trounce those around us who are striving toward the same goal, and this is where the difference between a culture of excellence and a culture of winning must shine through. For Christian leaders, recognizing the subtle distinction means the difference between building something that will fly high and far or something that will crash and burn on the launch pad.

Before we look at practical implications, let's ground this in the New Testament church experience. We know that Paul was a highly motivated man, both before and after his conversion. I also believe that part of his conversion process involved a fundamental change in his approach to building an organization. We see this in two sections of 1 Corinthians 3.

Brothers, I could not address you as spiritual but as worldly— mere infants in Christ. I gave you milk, not solid food, for you were not yet ready for it. Indeed, you are still not ready. You are still worldly. For since there is jealousy and quarreling among you, are you not worldly? Are you not acting like mere men? For when one says, "I follow Paul," and another, "I follow Apollos," are you not mere men?

What, after all, is Apollos? And what is Paul? Only servants, through whom you came to believe—as the Lord has assigned to each his task. I planted the seed, Apollos watered it, but God made it grow. So neither he who plants nor he who waters is anything, but only God, who makes things grow. The man who plants and the man who waters have one purpose, and each will be rewarded according to his own labor. For we are God's fellow workers; you are God's field, God's building.

vv. 1–9

Paul addresses a problem the Corinthian believers are having within their struggling nascent church. This serious issue keeps him from treating them as grown-up Christians, as spiritual leaders, and instead compels his view of them as infants who still need the basic, beginning teachings of the spiritual life, not able to ingest and digest the more mature aspects of the faith. What exactly is their deal? Simply put, *they're envious of each other.* In a spirit of competition, they've formed teams: the Paulines and the Apollosians. Who's the best in ministry? Who takes the prize in servanthood? Who whups the competition in total souls scored? Accomplishing spiritual goals by knockout isn't God's way.

To help his friends conquer this, Paul paints a completely different picture, detailing an alternative culture that by God's power can transform the ministry environment:

- He challenges the whole competitive paradigm; after all, they're on the same team.

- He suggests that each member has his own unique assignment, so their work is about accomplishing their assigned tasks rather than winning.

- He suggests a divinely appointed work flow (e.g., Paul plants and Apollos waters); a competitive spirit could break the God-ordained sequence of church building.

■ He points to Christ as the only true source of all accomplishment.

■ He emphasizes his mutual purpose with Apollos, according to their assigned tasks, for which God alone will reward.

■ He reminds them of their fellow-worker status.

Maybe you're thinking, "Okay, clearly Paul is challenging the oppositional paradigm. And yes, I suppose we ought to aim for cultures of excellence and quit trying to defeat our allies. But how are we going to motivate people if we don't have some good, friendly competition around here? Seems like we need to make comparisons and offer prizes to keep people excited and moving forward."

I hear you. And I've seen those prizes work effectively—for a while. But let's look at the alternative approach as Paul continues:

> By the grace God has given me, I laid a foundation as an expert builder, and someone else is building on it. But each one should be careful how he builds. For no one can lay any foundation other than the one already laid, which is Jesus Christ. If any man builds on this foundation using gold, silver, costly stones, wood, hay or straw, his work will be shown for what it is, because the Day will bring it to light. It will be revealed with fire, and the fire will test the quality of each man's work. If what he has built survives, he will receive his reward. If it is burned up, he will suffer loss; he himself will be saved, but only as one escaping through the flames.
>
> 1 CORINTHIANS 3:10–15

Notice that Paul doesn't become *un*motivated simply in moving beyond comparison and competition. He finishes this section by calling himself an *expert builder* and then emphasizes being careful about how we build. He points out that, in the end, Jesus will evaluate the quality of our work; the work we were assigned to do will be rewarded, while all other work will hit the fire. Here and in other texts (Philippians 3, for example), Paul stresses doing our best and calls us to excellence in carrying out kingdom assignments. *Yes, we're competing for a prize, but we can all win it together!* The standard is the God-given potential that's packaged with our heavenly calling—this is the sole basis of the rewards Jesus will hand us on that great Day ahead.

A TALE OF TWO CHURCHES

What about the business literature—does it lend support to the importance of distinguishing between cultures of excellence and cultures of winning? Yes! Jim Collins reflects upon how companies either focus on trying to beat the competition or on becoming great:

> *If you had the opportunity to sit down and read all 2,000+ pages of transcripts from the good-to-great interviews, you'd be struck by the utter absence of talk about "competitive strategy." Yes, they did talk about strategy, and they did talk about performance, and they did talk about becoming the best, and they even talked about winning. But they never talked in reactionary terms and never defined their strategies principally in response to what others were doing. They talked in terms of* what they were trying to create *and how they were trying to improve relative to an absolute standard of excellence.*[1]

Is this such a big deal? Before you answer, join me in thinking about a direct comparison I've been observing, an experience that's emphasized just how crucial it is to create a culture of excellence in the church while leaving competition in the locker room.

For ten years I watched two different churches build parallel ministries. "First Church of Anytown" began its process into this ministry with a BHAG (big hairy audacious goal) of *being better than anyone else.* The first (unstated) implication: "We must manipulate those around us and push our own strategy in every environment we enter." Strong vision flowed from up front, but the leaders consistently confessed difficulty with keeping people motivated. The vision had to be repeatedly re-shared and pounded home in order to sustain momentum.

Rather than candidly facing recurring problems, ministry leaders kept publicly reinforcing their success. This elicited a certain level of enthusiasm but closed them off to crucial feedback that could help them adjust and improve. Eventually, ministry results had to be "generated" to show progress toward the BHAG. When outside consultants provided extensive reports about what was *not* happening in the ministry, the leaders suppressed and concealed the findings. *Why would everyone else need to know about our behind-the-scenes speed bumps? Things might yet turn around . . .*

Not so. The problems escalated; energy finally had to be redeployed in other directions.

At this point, the senior leader became open to a different approach and hired new people to take over. About six months later, a friend from another church asked, "How are things going with that ministry?"

"It would have been better if that had never started," he replied. "I'd be much further along on several fronts if I weren't trying to rebuild from a disaster that's crumbling around a questionable goal: outrunning the competition."

As I mentioned, another congregation across the city—"Second Church of Thistown"—concurrently sought a dynamic ministry. They began by reviewing the best practices they'd gleaned from observing and analyzing other churches' experiences. They honestly didn't think about being better than anyone else. With deep passion for the work, they engaged as much of the congregation as possible, took ample feedback along the way, and regularly implemented changes in direction and method as they proceeded.

This ministry took plenty of time to gain momentum, but it gradually grew larger and larger. Leaders didn't start measuring until five years in; when they did, they compared their findings with a desire to include as much of the congregation as possible. When interacting with other teams, this team always sought to create win/win dynamics. In fact, they frequently sacrificed their own short-term goals for mutual long-term gain. These folks highly valued their sense of "one purpose" with all the ministries around them.

They also refused to overstate ministry facts or statistics, yet here's the mind-blowing irony: They inadvertently reached the BHAG that First Church of Anytown held so dear. What a surprise for these leaders! They could only give thanks to God and praise Him for His goodness ... as they continued seeking feedback, adjusting their tack, and garnering congregational participation.

The biggest difference? Motivation was rarely a problem in Second Church's ministry—everyone involved was thoroughly enthused and infused. Perhaps the best thing to say about it is, the ministry is still going strong and continues to be the core of the church in which it was built. The next leader won't be trying to reenergize a congregation damaged or devastated by the dubious benefits of competitive kingdom-building.

TAKE IT STEP BY STEP

When it comes to physical body image, it's easy to spot the difference between someone trying to look better than others and someone seeking the best physical conditioning possible. The whole cosmetic industry, for example, is built on the premise of *competing* good looks; shortcut diet plans and cosmetic plastic surgery are more about appearance than fitness.

Of course, most of us eventually come to the same sobering conclusion: There are no shortcuts with this; taking care of our bodies means focusing on being the best that we can be, not outdoing those around us.

In his chapter titled "The Flywheel and the Doom Loop," Jim Collins offers a helpful chart describing companies taking time to build something excellent versus companies striving for competitive victory:

HOW TO TELL IF YOU'RE ON THE FLYWHEEL
OR IN THE DOOM LOOP[2]

Signs That You're on the Flywheel (Good-to-Great Companies)	Signs That You're in the Doom Loop (Comparison Companies)
Follow a pattern of buildup leading to breakthrough.	Skip buildup and jump right to breakthrough.
Reach breakthrough by an accumulation of steps, one after the other, turn by turn of the flywheel; feels like an organic evolutionary process.	Implement big programs, radical change efforts, dramatic revolutions; chronic restructuring—always looking for a miracle moment or a new savior.
Confront the brutal facts to see clearly what steps *must* be taken to build momentum.	Embrace fads and engage in management hoopla, rather than confront the brutal facts.
Attain *consistency* with a clear Hedgehog Concept,[3] resolutely staying within the three circles.	Demonstrate chronic *inconsistency*—lurching back and forth and straying far outside the three circles.
Follow the pattern of disciplined people ("first who"), disciplined thought, disciplined action.	Jump right to action, without disciplined thought and without first getting the right people on the bus.
Harness appropriate technologies to your Hedgehog Concept to accelerate momentum.	Run about like Chicken Little in reaction to technology change, fearful of being left behind.
Make major acquisitions *after* breakthrough (if at all) to *accelerate* momentum.	Make major acquisitions *before* breakthrough in a doomed attempt to *create* momentum.

Spend little energy trying to motivate or align people; the momentum of the flywheel is infectious.	Spend a lot of energy trying to align and motivate people, rallying them around new visions.
Let results do most of the talking.	Sell the future to compensate for lack of results.
Maintain consistency over time; each generation builds on the work of previous generations; the flywheel continues to build momentum.	Demonstrate inconsistency over time; each new leader brings a radical new path; the flywheel grinds to a halt, and the doom loop begins anew.

Jim Collins, *Good to Great* (HarperCollins, 2001), pp. 183–184. Used by permission.

It's clear that purely competitive companies often end up in the Doom Loop; to avoid that result, one key is to get a handle on these principles for your own practical use. Let's try translating Jim's chart into a step-by-step process.

First, have your leadership team begin with what Collins calls the "Hedgehog Concept." That is, determine to focus on *one main thing* and do it well. Hedgehog organizations start at a single, focused point, the intersection of three recognitions (circles): what they're *passionate* about, what they're *talented* for, and what they can *effectively deliver* through ministry in their context. This delivers a defined concept of mission and vision within a given ministry or organization.

Second, either during or after this visioning process, focus on getting the right people in the right places (consult Chapter 4 on equipping).

Third, pray and think through the best way for your group to go about ministry and work together. Focus on becoming better and better at the process rather than jumping too fast or quickly accomplishing large results.

Fourth, let the process, and people's engagement with it, be the primary motivator rather than your ability to sell it in large motivational meetings.

Fifth, don't expect a big breakthrough or a magical moment to supercharge everything. Keep working on getting better and better at the ministry in front of you. Willingly seek feedback and honestly factor in the results so you can adjust accordingly at each step.

Sixth, as the ministry expands, add appropriate technology, people, and other resources to *enhance* momentum (not *create* it).

By way of contrast, let's consider: What would these steps look like in a "beat the competition" culture? First, the win-oriented leader tries a new idea and implements the fad that happens to be popular at the moment. Second, she quickly recruits anyone available and starts acting without thought for the unique situation's best ministry design. Third, she casts a big vision, with as many people as possible, rallying everyone around it. Fourth, she never seriously looks at the real results of feedback; rather, she keeps bringing back novel ideas and adding them to the mix. Fifth, she keeps restructuring, hoping for the long-awaited big breakthrough. Sixth, as the breakthrough apparently delays its breaking, she adds some technological gizmo to keep up with trends. (Finally, she gives her résumé frequent updates . . . just in case.)

THE BIG W: IT REALLY *ISN'T* EVERYTHING

There *is* a noncompetitive way to "do church."

I recall my involvement in re-visioning the men's ministry at my former church. Up to that point, the men kept to a tradition of holding breakfasts once a month, though attendance had dwindled to about twenty (a small number in a church with twenty-five hundred members). What vitalization could we now facilitate?

We started by planning a retreat together, focusing on the question "What would a great men's ministry look like—one that you'd want to join?" This allowed us to build our hedgehog concept (re-visioning our men's ministry) around four ideas, based on our passions:

(1) *Men gathering in a breakfast context just* once a quarter *(they were busy on Saturday mornings).*

(2) *Men gathering in small groups at least* twice a month *(up to once a week).*

(3) *Men doing service projects together in which their faith could be put into practical action at least* once a quarter.

(4) *Men going on travel adventures together—including ski retreats, golf outings, rafting trips, etc.*

Next we built a new team with diversely talented men. We brought on board two leaders, one with amazing administrative gifts and one who led a band (for music at the breakfasts). Around them were another ten men who played various roles: one ran the kitchen cooking crew; one did all the setup and takedown; one trained small-group leaders; one was connected to our missions ministry team; one produced graphics for the posters and flyers advertising our event speakers, and so on. Each breakfast would include an opportunity to join a small group, participate in a service opportunity, or go on an adventure. In addition, we gave the speakers for the four annual breakfasts an overarching theme that touched on different aspects of a man's life.

This team didn't set numerical targets, but evaluated each breakfast, retreat, and group, making alterations as they received input. And attendance numbers did increase! In year one, the breakfasts began to average around one hundred and twenty-five men. In year two, attendance jumped to one hundred and seventy-five. By year four, the breakfasts averaged three hundred and twenty-five with over five hundred men participating in small groups.

When a culture of excellence blossoms step by step, leaders will stay the course with the mission and vision they've been given. They will refuse to compete and compare, regardless of ministry's natural ups and downs. What evolves is the *unique specialization and diversification* that a given ministry or organization needs for its one-of-a-kind context.

This doesn't mean we can't learn from other contexts; on the contrary, the more good input and ideas the better. What it does mean, however, is that leaders don't just adopt someone else's model, willy-nilly, in order to be successful. They glean appropriate principles and apply them to what God has placed within their hearts. Thankfully, we Christian leaders have the Lord guiding us in the work we're called to do. We need not play the comparison game, for we are all one in His Spirit.

I began this chapter by inviting you into the world of sports to see what we could learn together about ministry. Don't assume I've lost my love for competitive play; I still have every ounce of respect for the famous Green Bay coach who spoke so much about winning. Vince Lombardi was a stalwart gridiron leader, having played the game himself on Fordham University's defensive front, known as the "Seven Blocks of Granite." I wouldn't want to try moving someone like him off the line when it comes to football.

This tough-talking man, who once studied for the priesthood, might forgive us if we paraphrase him for our purposes in the church: "Winning isn't everything; focus on *excellence.*" It's the difference between an organization that builds momentum far into the future and one doomed to spiral into nonexistence.

FOR REFLECTION

Use this space to write down your reflections, reactions, insights, and responses to this chapter and its central question.

Do we have a culture of excellence or a culture of winning?

SEVEN

Do You Play to Strengths So People Can Do Their Best?

As we've just seen, a culture of excellence, with people building a flywheel of competence, creates lasting effectiveness in organizations. One of the first steps, as Jim Collins puts it, is to "put the right people on the bus." It's become an important business theme—understanding exactly how leaders can get those right people on board.

Marcus Buckingham tackles this in his bestselling *First, Break All the Rules*[1] and *Now, Discover Your Strengths* (with Donald O. Clifton).[2] In the introduction to the latter, he comments on just how much work we must do in effective recruitment, placement, and people-development.

In Gallup's total database of more than 1.7 million employees, in 101 companies from 63 countries, we have asked the "opportunity to do your best" question. What percentage do you think strongly agrees that they have an opportunity to do what they do best every day? . . .

Globally, only 20% of employees working in the large organizations we surveyed feel that their strengths are in play every day. Most bizarre of all, the longer an employee stays with an organization, and the higher he climbs the traditional ladder, the less likely he is to strongly agree that he is playing to his strengths.[3]

Buckingham goes on to point out that the reason organizations often fail to play to their employees' strengths is that they've held two flawed assumptions about people: (1) Each person can learn to be competent in almost anything, and (2) each person's greatest room for growth lies in his or her areas of greatest weakness. George Gallup's work challenges and disputes both commonly held misconceptions, as does the following scriptural presentation.

Each one should use whatever gift he has received to serve others, faithfully administering God's grace in its various forms. If anyone speaks, he should do it as one speaking the very words of God. If anyone serves, he should do it with the strength God provides, so that in all things God may be praised through Jesus Christ.
1 PETER 4:10–11

WHY NOT FOLLOW THE BIBLICAL WAY?

The Bible teaches that each of us is uniquely created, with no two of us exactly alike. Building on the 1 Peter text, a Christian worldview brings these realities to the table: (1) A person's *gifts* are enduring and unique, and (2) a person's *strengths* indicate the place for greatest growth. Christian leaders need to ask, then: *Why don't we consistently fill ministry positions based upon gifts and strengths?* I've noticed three troubling obstacles that often hinder us.

RECRUITING BY RELATIONSHIP

We base our volunteering or hiring decisions primarily on "relational fit" rather than a person's talents and gifts. Many leaders fall into this trap by the very nature of who they are, not out of some nefarious motive. After all, we Christians already enjoy a special connection through the indwelling Spirit; we have a shared faith, and our common worldview tends to create a relational connection. However, when faced with a volunteering or hiring decision, we need to be objective about the competencies and abilities needed. If we hire someone simply because we get along with her so well, we may soon be looking for ways to replace her.

I've observed many such scenarios over the past few months, one when I consulted a church where standard procedure is to interview candidates within the congregation when paid staff positions open. "We want to empower the body of Christ," they explain, "and lift up people within their own worshiping community." They have excellent motives. They love people. But in their informal approach, they've never gotten around to drawing up job descriptions, with accountabilities and core competencies clearly detailed. Consequently, people haven't been hired for their ability to do the job, but for their sense of fitting in.

When I arrived on the scene, they'd suffered through a whole decade of mismatches between ministries and ministers. I saw long-term pain for those hired, general discord in the congregation, lack of success in ministry, and an overriding dissatisfaction with performance outcomes. No fun!

Consider another manifestation of relational employing, which happens in the name of "being a community and not just a corporation" or "being gracious." Thus a staff allows a person to continue working in a position he has proven unable to undertake or uphold. Yes, it may seem more gracious, more loving to do this, and, for a while, it can be the right thing to do (we accept failure *within limits*). But there does come a point where it's anything but helpful to enable ongoing, unchanging incompetence.

Although I disagree with many of management guru Jack Welch's practices, I do like this idea: It is *not* better to keep honest feedback and consequences from an employee. If he's in his late thirties, for example, and continues in mediocrity (or worse) for a full decade, you now have a person in his late forties who is virtually unemployable once he's finally let go. Only consistent and truthful feedback about performance keeps people sharp and developing in their competencies. Furthermore, if needed, it gives them the earliest opportunity to make a change that will produce a better fit for them.

FINDING THE FAVORITE

Leaders sometimes hire based on one or another type of favoritism. Maybe you're related to the new church secretary, for instance. What a coincidence! Or maybe your friend *really* needs a job (think of those poor kids). Or it'd be nice to have the mayor serving on your building committee, or . . . can you think of a few more tempting favorites?

When I serve as a consultant, this element often slowly seeps into my consciousness. As I'm introduced to staff members, for example, it begins to dawn on me that there are myriad similar last names, many mentions of "in-law," and addresses in the same corner of town (if not the same street . . . or the same house).

I realize that sometimes this can be appropriate. Most of the time, however, it's an abuse of ministry positions. Believing the classic assumption that a person can learn to be competent in almost anything, these churches bypass the discipline of defining the work. They also fail to undertake the discernment process about who God is calling to minister in a particular position.

The worst part is observing the results. First, many of those watching the system know exactly what's happening, so they live with constant mistrust. Second, if the favoritism-based match isn't a good one, it ends up being painful and divisive for the family or friends involved. The ultimate dream of "ministering together" is rarely brought about by this arrangement.

Having worked with many family-owned businesses that lose their cutting edge through similar mistakes, I know the importance of paying close attention when making this type of hire. In most cases, people connected in various ways *should* still be given equal opportunity to apply for positions; however, an independent group of people, committed to discerning what God wants and what's best for the institution, should make the final decisions. Whoever is hired can then know that the choice was based on competence.

> *My brothers, as believers in our glorious Lord Jesus Christ, don't show favoritism. Suppose a man comes into your meeting wearing a gold ring and fine clothes, and a poor man in shabby clothes also comes in. If you show special attention to the man wearing fine clothes and say, "Here's a good seat for you," but say to the poor man, "You stand there" or "Sit on the floor by my feet," have you not discriminated among yourselves and become judges with evil thoughts?*
> JAMES 2:1–4

PEOPLE-ING TO PLEASE

Some church leaders (consciously or unconsciously) recruit people based upon their own need to please an individual or group within the congregation. Putting a short-term Band-Aid over a long-term relational or political battle spells disaster for everyone involved. A story from my history will illustrate.

It was an evangelical church that grew very large, adding diverse types of believers to its numbers. One part of the congregation began to value a particular set of social issues, making those pet perspectives a litmus test for Christian faithfulness. They became vocal and even somewhat pushy in attempting to influence congregational opinion.

As often happens when such groups get out of control, this one tried to obtain positions of power and influence such as those on the nominating committees. They deployed "secret agent" candidates and began lobbying; when they succeeded—with the majority of the congregation disagreeing—the results were predictable and disastrous. Talent, vision, and values succumbed to people-pleasing. A divided congregation faced a painful future.

No wonder Paul warns against embracing the world's way:

> *Do not conform any longer to the pattern of this world, but be transformed by the renewing of your mind. Then you will be*

able to test and approve what God's will is—his good, pleasing
and perfect will. For by the grace given me I say to every one of
you: Do not think of yourself more highly than you ought, but
rather think of yourself with sober judgment, in accordance
with the measure of faith God has given you. Just as each of us
has one body with many members, and these members do not
all have the same function, so in Christ we who are many form
one body, and each member belongs to all the others. We have
different gifts, according to the grace given us. If a man's gift is
prophesying, let him use it in proportion to his faith. If it is
serving, let him serve; if it is teaching, let him teach; if it is
encouraging, let him encourage; if it is contributing to the needs
of others, let him give generously; if it is leadership, let him gov-
ern diligently; if it is showing mercy, let him do it cheerfully.
ROMANS 12:1–8

Paul's whole point is to challenge a mentality that believes people
can do and can become anything they desire. We all have roles, yes,
but these must draw upon our talents and gifts. Marcus Buckingham and the Gallup organization have discovered how powerful it
is for an organization to begin thinking this way, hiring and developing people according to their strengths:

When employees answered that they strongly agree with the
statement that they are "able to do what they do best every
day," they were 50% more likely to work in business units with
lower employee turnover, 38% more likely to work in more pro-
ductive business units, and 44% more likely to work in business
units with higher customer satisfaction.[4]

So what's the basic equation for creating competence? Here's
my suggestion:

Gifts + knowledge + skills + experience = competence.

This is a basic template to utilize in writing job descriptions for important volunteer positions *and* paid staff positions. Here's the equation in the form of questions you could use in the process:

- What spiritual gifts and natural talents do we need for this position?

- What knowledge base would help this person succeed?

- What skills will enhance this person's effectiveness?

- What experience best prepares an individual for this work?

After writing the job descriptions, you can use these same questions to evaluate the candidates considering the job. Or make sure the people who recruit possible volunteers for your ministries use them regularly.[5]

MAXIMIZE STRENGTH, MANAGE WEAKNESS

After interviewing thousands of top supervisors in diverse fields, Gallup discovered not only how to hire people according to their strengths but also how to *develop* them more effectively. The research identified four stages ("base camps") that employees and volunteers traverse in the process of becoming fully engaged with an organization. Each stage must follow upon the previous one or a person will remain stuck.

Stage #1: The person needs to know what he is to do and be given the materials and equipment needed to do it.

Stage #2: At this point, contribution to and growth within the organization now become important to the person. Sometimes very quickly, and sometimes over a period of time, she begins to look for ways that her talents can have an impact in a significant way in the organization.

Stage #3: After a person knows what is expected and can see possibilities for personal impact and growth, the "people dimension" becomes important. He cares about co-workers and about the organization's general culture.

Stage #4: Finally at the last stage, the person knows what's expected of her, knows she's contributing significantly, and knows she fits in at all levels of the organization. Now her concerns turn to long-term growth.

Team leaders and staff supervisors can easily use these four stages of engagement to keep tabs on those they're overseeing. Being aware that different members of their teams are in different stages of engagement with the ministry, they can frame the right questions and respond to different individual issues. For example, a brand-new person may simply be wondering, "What is this job anyway?" A person deeper into the engagement process wants to know: "Can I really contribute around here with my unique perspectives and ideas?" Still further into the process, another individual may wonder, "Where is my work here going in the long term?" The four stages help us fully involve individuals at different points in the process.

Supervisors (pastors and layleaders) can also nurture such development if they know how to properly handle people's strengths and weaknesses. As Gallup discovered: *Great supervisors do not try to strengthen weaknesses; instead, they maximize strengths while managing around weaknesses.* When organizations send people for training and development, they are usually attempting to strengthen people's weaknesses. The result? They end up with well-developed weaknesses!

Is that really the kind of person we want working for us? A person who has finally honed her weaknesses up to the level of mediocrity? (Remember: Weaknesses are often simply *areas of non-talent.*) Wouldn't it be smarter to fully develop people's strengths?

Recall the year when Michael Jordan worked hard at baseball. He spent hour upon hour in batting cages, countless afternoons shagging fly balls, and dedicated himself to mastering bunting and base-running techniques. All of that in order to become ... an *average* minor leaguer. Jordan, of course, was born for basketball. Honing his court skills over the years, he became the greatest ever.

While maximizing strengths, suppose we were to manage *around* weaknesses or non-talent? This is exactly what great supervisors do by instinct. They steer Michael Jordan away from the ballpark and point him to the gym. It's much more effective to keep adding knowledge, skills, and experience in a person's area of strength, managing *around* non-strengths. In 2 Peter, we see the importance of a "culture of development" as suggested by Gallup's research.

> *Make every effort to add to your faith goodness; and to goodness, knowledge; and to knowledge, self-control; and to self-control, perseverance; and to perseverance, godliness; and to godliness, brotherly kindness; and to brotherly kindness, love. For if you possess these qualities in increasing measure, they will keep you from being ineffective and unproductive in your knowledge of our Lord Jesus Christ.*
> 2 PETER 1:5–8

Peter's list of admonishments for believers to "add to" or develop themselves includes categories of knowledge, character, relationships, emotional intelligence, etc. The product is suggested in the final sentence: *When we develop as Christians—"in increasing measure"—we become more effective and productive.*

In *Promoting a Developmental Culture in Your Organization*, Peggy Simonsen describes what many people are experiencing in today's less hierarchical and standardized organizations: the need to be persistently learning and constantly updating skills and knowledge. She outlines many useful ways to meet this need while offering a series of concrete situations that require development in twenty-first-century organizations. In our organizations, we need to help people to

■ overcome barriers;

- build their strengths;

- create a better fit;

- achieve greater satisfaction;

- expand existing skill sets;

- encourage accomplishments;

- create new challenges;

- prepare for a desired future level of responsibility;

- prepare for a future move.[6]

All these needs occur in individuals within organizations. The idea is to create a process that keeps volunteers and employees developing over time. Therefore, many organizations are wisely creating development plans right alongside performance reviews. Couldn't the church do something similar? Here are some possible ways:

- Offer regular developmental courses and workshops.

- Schedule team retreats and conferences.

- Assign readings or online instruction.

- Establish contact with a mentor who can train and guide.

- Give frequent feedback about results (and record learnings).

- Visit best-practice institutions of parallel scope and direction.

- Encourage memberships in professional groups.

- Provide new job-description challenges to tackle.

The list can go on and on, and I'm sure you have your own suggestions. The big idea is to continue to develop your staff, employees, or volunteers over time. Continue to activate their full engagement in the organization. Maximize their strengths so they have the opportunity to do their best.

IT'S ALL ABOUT YOUR LOVES

What ever motivates us to hire and develop for reasons other than talent and fit? In *The Four Loves,* C. S. Lewis argues that we human beings face a phenomenal internal war: a competition of "loves" that battle for sovereignty in our souls. Sometimes romantic love sits at the center of our being. Sometimes friendship or family takes that central place. These are false infinites, inordinate affections. Unless love for God takes up its rightful place in our hearts, any other love goes from asset to enemy and will work against the Spirit's purposes.

Other loves never fully achieve their God-imitating masquerade and leave damage in their wake.

The claim to divinity which our loves so easily make can be refuted without going so far as that. The loves prove that they are unworthy to take the place of God by the fact that they cannot even remain themselves and do what they promise to do without God's help.[7]

Because a leader's misplaced love can set up a misguided hire, we need to face ourselves squarely: Why do we *need* to hire this person sitting before us? Does he clearly have the gifts and calling for the ministry? Or is some need within ourselves motivating the decision? Hopefully, God's love is orchestrating and managing all the other loves within us.

In this context, the difficult-to-grasp Luke 14:26 makes sense:

If anyone comes to me and does not hate his father and mother, his wife and children, his brothers and sisters—yes, even his own life—he cannot be my disciple.

In other words, choosing to put God's love first in our hearts will keep us from *inappropriately favoring* even those we love deeply. Therefore, Lewis concludes:

> *The real question is which, when the decision comes, do you choose to put first? Which love will claim your will, in the last resort?*[8]

FOR REFLECTION

Use this space to write down your reflections, reactions, insights, and responses to this chapter and its central question.

Do I look for, develop, and play to strengths so people can do their best?

EIGHT

Are You Really a Team?

When some missionaries in the Philippines set up a croquet game in their yard, several of their Agta neighbors became interested and wanted to join the fun. The missionaries explained the rules and started them out, each with a mallet and ball. As they progressed, the opportunity came for one player to knock another's ball out of play, but an explanation of procedure only puzzled him. "Why would I want to knock out his ball?" he asked.

"So you will be the one to win!" the missionary gushed. The short-statured man, clad only in a loincloth, shook his head in bewilderment.

The game continued, no one following the advice. When a player successfully got through all the wickets, his game wasn't over—he went back and gave aid and advice to the others. As the final player moved toward the last wicket, the affair was a team effort, and finally, when the last wicket was played, the "team" shouted happily: "We won! We won!"[1]

You see, competition is generally untenable in a hunting and gathering society, where people survive not by competing but by sharing equally in every activity. Isn't that how the church, Christ's body, should be? We're a team; we all win together. Right alongside development of individuals in organizations, leaders also need to develop the health and depth of ministry teams.

The question that so easily follows, however, is: "How do we create great teams that actually function and deliver as they promise?" Bestselling author Patrick Lencioni has written exceptionally on this in *Overcoming the Five Dysfunctions of a Team*. These are his words about the power and promise of teamwork:

> *As difficult as teamwork is to measure and achieve, its power cannot be denied. When people come together and set aside their individual needs for the good of the whole, they can accomplish what might have looked impossible on paper. They can do this by eliminating the politics and confusion that plague most organizations. As a result, they get more done in less time and with less cost. I think that's worth a lot of effort.*[2]

While altogether eliminating politics and confusion would be nice, most of us in churches or ministry organizations have experienced both the good and the bad with teams. When they're good, they're wonderfully effective, creating joy and blessing for all involved. When they're bad, they cause heartache, create distrust and ill will, and leave some folks wounded for years.

WHICH TEAM WOULD YOU ENJOY?

Let me tell you the tale of two teams, which I'll call Team One and Team Two. They're actually composites of good and bad teams I've experienced over the years.

The members of Team One had a glaring problem, obvious from the beginning: They had a hard time being the least bit vulnerable with each other. A few weeks after I joined, I asked one member, "Is it all right to be *not okay* on this team?"

"Sure, if you don't talk about it here. And if you go away somewhere, and deal with it quickly, so you can come back *okay*."

But sometimes we aren't okay. That we're *human* means we experience ups and downs, foibles and idiosyncrasies, weaknesses and sins. Shouldn't team members be able to acknowledge these with one another? Could we be ready to lift each other up when our not-okay-ness starts to get the best of us?

In Team One, the answer was *no*. Consequently, whenever real conflict needed to happen (and sometimes we really do need honest and direct confrontation in order to solve problems), it never did. One consultant observed members constantly cutting each other down outside meetings. The upshot was a total lack of commitment to the team. After all, why would people want to open themselves to the potential hurt of such a saber-swirling environment? Bottom line for Team One members: Make sure your own turf is protected and no one is blocking your personal objectives.

Accountability? No one would come through in a team effort, even though long lists of goals, with accompanying deadlines, filled the meeting minutes. Every time these goals were reviewed, new dates would be attached to push them further into the future. People worked at advancing their careers while caring little for teamwork. Turnover was constant. Futility reigned.

Now let's look at a refreshing contrast. Team Two comprised individuals who'd accepted each other in their differences, both strong points and shortcomings. Consequently, when they were together, they interacted openly and honestly. If there was a conflict issue brewing, it was raised in the group and dealt with; the accompanying feelings, whether anger, fear, hurt, or sadness, could be handled. The members seemed to sense that if they could work together in the midst of such emotions they'd be opening the floodgates to joy as well.

It wasn't important that any one person got his way; instead, all points of view were considered. After they hashed through their decisions, they'd set a direction that everyone could buy into because they'd committed to the greater vision rather than just their own personal piece of the pie. Accountability was easy because everyone focused on the same goals. The team's accomplishments were both individually and corporately outstanding. A typical comment that constantly emanated: "There's a lot of love flowing here."

Lencioni mentions in his introduction that team-building doesn't involve lots of complex ideas but rather firm commitment:

> *Teamwork is extremely hard to achieve. It can't be bought, and it can't be attained by hiring an intellectual giant from the world's best business school. It requires levels of courage and discipline—and emotional energy—that even the most driven executives don't always possess.*[3]

READY TO MAKE SOME PROGRESS?

Lencioni outlines a virtual road map to creating great teams. In the diagram below, you can see a definite *progression* toward that destination. Functional teams grow into being as they move toward

THE FIVE DYSFUNCTIONS OF A TEAM

Overcoming the Five Dysfunctions of a Team, Patrick Lencioni; copyright © 2005 by Patrick Lencioni. Reprinted with permission of John Wiley & Sons, Inc.

the top of the pyramid; that is, as they eliminate the five *dys*functional obstacles.

BUILDING TRUST

Teamwork grows upon a foundation of trust, and trust requires a combination of (1) willingness to be vulnerable and (2) acquiring deeper understanding into each member (especially valuing individual uniquenesses). Lencioni often uses the Myers-Briggs Type Indicator to help accomplish the latter; through analyzing and sharing about their MBTI scores, members come to value one another's strengths. The combination of understanding uniqueness and embracing vulnerability works wonders in transforming team dynamics from fear to trust. People begin to be real; political game-playing withers away; hiding and defending become unnecessary.

ALLOWING CONFLICT

As trust deepens, members begin to risk open disagreement and conflict in team interactions. This is critical to problem-solving, of course, let alone valuable in building cohesion. When team members *genuinely* interact about decisions and problems, they make real progress toward team goals. No longer do the discussions stay at a surface level for fear of hurting someone's feelings. There's a sense that "Hey, we can deal with any possible hurt! It's okay, because in caring for the team, we care for one another." Relationships move to a more intimate level because the team has willingly set ground rules for conflict engagement. They know that conflict will occasionally bubble up, so they've prepared themselves for moving through it via healthy interaction.

BUYING IN

Let's assume that all team members are being heard and that their ideas are being soberly considered by all. Now when it comes time to commit to a particular direction, everyone is much more likely to buy in. Even when an individual disagrees with the group's conclusion, she commits, knowing that her own point of view has been duly weighed.

BEING ACCOUNTABLE

When genuine buy-in happens, accountability to group goals becomes possible. Why? Because everyone has consented to the established goals. Now a team must build on established trust by keeping each other accountable to these joint commitments.

MONITORING RESULTS

In this environment of wholehearted accountability, the team can focus its energies on results; cooperative achievement has become more attainable. Rewarding and reviewing both individual and team goals will keep this focus on overall objectives.

TEAMWORK REQUIRES "ONE ANOTHER"

Hidden in this wonderful model of teamwork are a series of pivot points upon which its success hinges. These are places we reach in the journey toward synergistic ministry, places where we could go one way or the other. Pivot points are fork-in-the-road areas that can take a team forward in progress or cause them to step back from healthy function into the land of dysfunction.

In general, this approach to team-building requires a *desire to be in relationship with one another*. The New Testament gives us guidance in offering a series of one-anothering commands meant to flesh out what this actually means; many reside exactly at the crucial crossroads in Lencioni's team-building model.

THE PIVOT POINT OF ACCEPTING *OR* JUDGING

Which way will a team go when it's invited to see and accept one another with the rose-colored glasses removed? As members begin risking vulnerability and start honestly sharing about themselves, others have a choice to respond. They can accept one another, weaknesses and all, or they can pass judgment.

Paul faced groups in the Roman church who were at odds with each other over what he called "disputable matters." Hear his words in this regard:

> *Accept him whose faith is weak, without passing judgment on disputable matters. One man's faith allows him to eat everything, but another man, whose faith is weak, eats only vegetables. The man who eats everything must not look down on him who does not, and the man who does not eat everything must not condemn the man who does, for God has accepted him.*
>
> *Who are you to judge someone else's servant? To his own master he stands or falls. And he will stand, for the Lord is able to make him stand.*
>
> ROMANS 14:1–4

If team members don't practice such acceptance, trust won't develop among them. Not only will members stop being vulnerable, they'll also be markedly cautious about entering into legitimate conflict or sharing what they're truly thinking. On the other hand, if teams choose acceptance, then a continual openness is possible, and the next pivot point comes into view. . . .

THE PIVOT POINT OF LISTENING *OR* RAGING

As people freely begin to disagree and share differing perspectives, the wisdom of the apostle James comes into play.

> *My dear brothers, take note of this: Everyone should be quick to listen, slow to speak and slow to become angry.*
>
> 1:19

We need our teamwork pervaded by a kind and compassionate atmosphere, one in which members truly believe that everybody's point of view is at least worth hearing. When feelings get hurt, this healthy team can move toward forgiving one another, as necessary, and then moving on. They're devoted to process, knowing that active listening forms the groundwork of every good relationship. They listen—*really* listen, not just with the ears but with the heart. They decline to take things personally, refuse to light the fires of internal rage.

THE PIVOT POINT OF SUBMITTING *OR* DEFYING

The free exchange of ideas must eventually culminate in actual decisions. At times a consensus arises—great! At other times the leader will need to make a decision, or it might require a vote and majority rule. Thus a team arrives at another critical pivot point on the journey to healthy functioning, and here Paul can speak to us again:

> *Submit to one another out of reverence for Christ.*
> EPHESIANS 5:21

> *Love must be sincere. Hate what is evil; cling to what is good.*
> *Be devoted to one another in brotherly love. Honor one another*
> *above yourselves. Never be lacking in zeal, but keep your spiri-*
> *tual fervor, serving the Lord.*
> ROMANS 12:9–11

Only as members focus on submitting to team process—and honoring others above themselves—will they be able to move forward fully committed. A member can choose this pathway even when he doesn't agree with the overall specific direction—difficult, yes, but an admirable act of humility out of reverence for Christ. And this full buy-in is the only way accountability will have substance—when the team begins to hold *all* its members accountable to the commitments they're making together. When a team *fully* buys in, its members are saying: "I'm prepared to respond both to encouragement and correction in achieving the goals we've set together." The other pathway, leading back to dysfunction, causes a member to say (either outwardly or inwardly, with a "nice" demeanor): "I'm *not* going along with their program; I'm holding out for my own way."

THE PIVOT POINT OF TRUTH-TELLING *OR* PEACEKEEPING

Even for those who trust one another, this can be a tough crossroads to reach: *Will I speak the painful truth or cover it over to "avoid a scene"?*

> *Speaking the truth in love, we will in all things grow up into him who is the Head, that is, Christ.*
> EPHESIANS 4:15

We all want to avoid ugly scenes! But Paul knew we wouldn't fully grow into Christ's body unless we're honest with one another. Have you developed this ability? If you're a team leader, it's crucial, because if you haven't actualized this, people will become discouraged by the constant guessing: What's *really* going on here? What's he *really* thinking? What's she *really* trying to hint at?

David Augsburger, in his classic *Caring Enough to Confront*, offers these relevant words:

> *Truth and love are the two necessary ingredients for any relationship with integrity. Love—because all positive relationships begin with friendship, appreciation, respect. And truth—because no relationship of trust can long grow from dishonesty, deceit, betrayal; it springs up from the solid stuff of integrity. . . . These are the two arms of genuine relationship: Confrontation with truth. Affirmation with love.*
>
> *I grow most rapidly when a brother supports me with the arm of loving respect, then confronts me with the arm of clear honesty. Confronting and caring bring growth. Confrontation plus acceptance equals growth. This is how God relates to us.*[4]

THE PIVOT POINT OF MERELY ACTING *OR* ACHIEVING

The final step in Lencioni's model is to stay focused on the team's results. Members still need to be reminded of the targets toward which they're collectively aiming. Are they truly achieving their goals? For a biblical correlation: "Let us consider how we may spur one another on toward love and good deeds" (Hebrews 10:24). If Scripture says that actual *deeds* flow from holy attitudes, should we want any less?

Again, in the healthy team, members have an overriding desire to be in relationship. As we've noted, becoming this type of team will require courage, discipline, and a commitment to living out the Bible's one-anothering commands. This creates the possibility of people transcending their own agendas for the good—the *success*—of the team!

Let's close with a return to our body analogy. When any part of the human body does not submit to the integrated processes of the whole, it becomes, literally, cancerous to the entire organism. Cancer, at its core, is the disease of out-of-control cells. Individual cells reproduce and outgrow their appropriate boundaries, beginning to overstep beyond their legitimate expression of growth. *Cancer cells have no sense of working with the other teams of cells around them—in effect they pursue a personal growth agenda.*

As scientists have probed deeper into the mechanisms of cancer formation, they've discovered a breakdown of "communication skills" in the receptors on cancer cell membranes. Cancer cells do not experience the feedback of other cells designed to link up with them; cancer cells don't do teamwork.

In like manner, people who don't trust each other—and therefore never give and receive honest feedback or interact openly—never feel a sense of team with others. Tragically, they become focused on getting more turf for themselves.

In his book *Wind and Fire,* Bruce Larson[5] tells of a bird-loving friend who lives near Hoyt Park in Madison, Wisconsin. Invariably, in all seasons, his yard is filled with all kinds of birds; however, squirrels have continually plagued his feeders. Exasperated, he finally bought a pellet gun and began to shoot them, two and three a day, every day, week after week. In spite of these desperate measures, the squirrel population seemed undiminished.

One day, while he was discussing the irksome problem with a colleague, his friend said, "I solved that problem. I was troubled by squirrels too, but now I trap them. I trap two or three a day and take them down to Hoyt Park and release them."

Larson comments: "That's an example of what can happen when we approach all of our problems individually, with no sense of the larger picture." Which brings us back to Lencioni's poignant question: *Are you really a team?*

If you're a team leader, it might be best for you to hear it phrased thus: Are you truly committed to doing the work—with the necessary emotional commitment, courage, and discipline—to build a true sense of *team* among your members? Your response can make the difference between an achieving, synergistic work force and a cancerous conglomeration of individual strugglers.

FOR REFLECTION

Use this space to write down your reflections, reactions, insights, and responses to this chapter and its central question.

Are we really a team?

NINE

Are You Ready to Create New Wineskins?

Structural changes can be good . . . or not so good. As the old story goes: It seems the oarsmen on the ancient ship had been complaining about their long hours of toil, rowing, rowing, day after day, in the sweaty underbelly below decks. They begged for change. Then came the day when the Oar Master appeared with a startling announcement. "Gentlemen, I have good news and bad news," he began. "First the good: From now on, we'll have a change of underwear *every day.*" The men slumped with relief. Their workday would definitely be more pleasant. "Now for the bad news," he continued. "Schwartz, you change with Santini. Miller, you change with O'Leary. . . ."

Would you agree that the "new" is not always so good? Newness purely for the sake of innovation is indeed suspect. But what if the new follows from the "old" of Scripture? It can only do the church good to go back to biblical organizational principles. In fact, this is the whole purpose of all we've explored so far—to learn and apply Christ-based leadership in order to build a biblically based church structure and function. (When any of the secular research fits this model and helps us along, all the better!) I hope you've picked up on the overarching themes related to this outcome: the centrality of great teams, the need for empowered people, the leadership skills and character required for success.

All of this intends to shift the focus of organizational energy from a top-down hierarchy to a leveled, organic community working from the inside out and outside in. This way, the focus is on the outer circle, where ministry occurs, rather than on the inner, as in a traditional organization. Howard Snyder, pastor and church-renewal visionary, who wrote decades ago about structure, firmly believed it was a movement back to scriptural basics, a transition that makes all the difference in congregational health.

> *A church which intends to grow and serve the kingdom of God must be structured in harmony with the biblical understanding of the church. This is not to say that a church structured otherwise will not grow, for churches with the most diverse structures have obviously grown and survived. But a church not structured in harmony with biblical principles will never achieve the quality of growth and authenticity of discipleship, which God intends.*
>
> *In itself, church structure is neither evil nor illegitimate. The question concerns the kinds of structures that best serve the church in its life and witness. Particular structures will be legitimate or illegitimate depending not only on what they are intended to accomplish, but on their function—what they actually do accomplish.*[1]

Regarding these two types of congregation (or organization), the diagram represents the key large-scale contrasts.

READY FOR A SERIOUS STRUCTURE SHIFT?

In *The Individualized Corporation,* Sumantra Ghoshal and Christopher Bartlett outline how this shift plays out in detail. They suggest, first of all, that each layer of an organization is called to think differently about its *roles.* In simple terms, they suggest that

■ frontline implementers think of themselves as innovative entre-preneurs;

■ administrative controllers think of themselves as developmental coaches;

■ strategic architects think of themselves as institution builders.[2]

In *traditional organizations,* vision and direction come from the strategic architects at the center. The vision then sifts down into var-ious departments (or areas of ministry) where classic committees

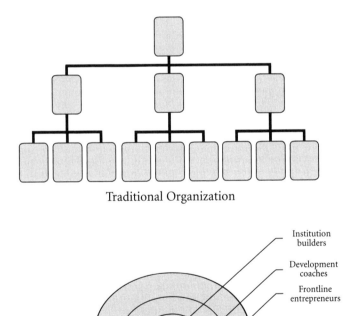

Traditional Organization

Institution builders

Development coaches

Frontline entrepreneurs

Organic Organization

receive administrative control over that part of the work. The lay-leaders or associate pastors thus have administrative control over particular areas, recruiting volunteers to be the frontline imple-menters of the tasks each area is to accomplish in ministry.

In *organic organizations,* by contrast, the innovation happens in the outer ring, where laypeople in ministry teams work at the entrepreneurial edge. Layleaders and associate pastors serve pri-marily as developmental coaches for these teams; these leaders, in turn, meet with the church's (or organization's) senior leaders, who are building an institution in which more and more teams can be released into ministry.

If you're wondering whether this might be just a matter of semantics, my response is to invite you to look a little closer. In the paragraphs that follow, I believe you'll see important distinguishing implications as to role definition and processes. It's more than words; it's about structuring for ministry so that Christ's body can function with health and vitality.

But, again, you may ask, "Is this kind of structural change really necessary to live out our calling in the church?" I believe it *is* nec-essary to live out the vision of leadership that's been suggested all along in this book. This vision flows directly from scriptural man-dates like these words of Jesus about structuring—and restructur-ing—for ministry:

> No one tears a patch from a new garment and sews it on an old one. If he does, he will have torn the new garment, and the patch from the new will not match the old. And no one pours new wine into old wineskins. If he does, the new wine will burst the skins, the wine will run out and the wineskins will be ruined. No, new wine must be poured into new wineskins. And no one after drinking old wine wants the new, for he says, "The old is better."
> LUKE 5:36–39

For our focus, I draw at least three implications.

First, straightforwardly, new wine causes old wineskins to rupture, wasting the wine and destroying the wineskins; it must be stored in new wineskins.

Second, those who have tasted old wine don't think the new wine tastes better.

Third, it's not enough to mend the old wineskin for reinforcement—a new wineskin is the only solution. In terms of our organizations, we're talking about leadership that unfolds within an organically functioning body. Leaders must be prepared for what this newness will mean, over time.

Why? Because this way of leading will require new structures to contain the new energy and direction that emerge. Leaders must be convinced that a patch job won't be enough; they must think in terms of Jesus' radical calling, which is a structural redesign. All the while they'll be caring for those accustomed to mechanistic leadership; they must nurture these folks with all wisdom and gentleness, for these are the sheep who will never fully appreciate innovative organizational design, and though for them the old wine will always taste a little better, they need not be left behind.

HOW DOES ORGANIC MINISTRY LOOK IN THE CHURCH?

I saw firsthand the contrast of the new and old wineskins when I attended a Presbyterian church—in its place of origin, the British Isles—and compared it to certain dynamic Presbyterian churches I'd seen in the U.S. (This only *symbolizes* the old and new world, of course, and doesn't represent all churches in either country.) In the "old wineskin," I attended a meeting of the ruling leaders, called the "session."

In this church, you were ordained for life, and all forty elders were there (out of eighty church members, total). Their average age was sixty-five, and the clerk of the session was their most senior. The pastor led the meeting by strictly applying Robert's Rules of Order. There was no discussion. There was very little human interaction. The meeting opened and closed with prayer, and then everyone went home.

None of the three processes—entrepreneurial, integrative, or renewal—had occurred in this church for decades. The congregation was simply wasting away . . . in an *orderly* fashion.

I also attended an American church in which all three processes were functioning at full strength. Laypeople in ministry teams worked at the cutting edge of entrepreneurial ministry. Layleaders and associate pastors acted as coaches, resourcing, recruiting, developing, and holding members accountable while integrating the various ministries. The senior leadership established vision and values, constantly keeping their minds on the cultural horizon so they'd be ready to make needed changes for the future.

What a leadership contrast!

If they are to stay vital and grow over time, organizations need these three kinds of health-inducing processes—from the new-wine structure—unfolding within them:

- *An Entrepreneurial Process.* Members, teams, and leaders constantly seek to create new ministries (or expand and adapt old ones) to serve new contexts, audiences, or segments of the congregation or community.

- *An Integrative Process.* The structure integrates all departments or teams so no one is stepping on another's work; all are moving in one direction, becoming a cohesive, seamless whole.

- *A Renewal Process.* The organization implements redesign projects in response to major cultural or marketplace shifts, refocusing on the contemporary factors and demands that require attention.

Each of the *processes* in the chart above requires a different set of functions from the three *roles* we described earlier.[3] Let's look at how each role must function in order to help each process unfold effectively within congregations or organizations.

THE ENTREPRENEURIAL PROCESS

To create new ministries or expand existing ones, frontline ministry teams must constantly pursue new opportunities. For this to happen well, coaches (usually layleaders or associate pastors) must be developing individuals by recruiting, training, and placing more and more on teams. They also must be reviewing the direction and results of existing teams while facilitating vision and providing support.

Coaches help team members hold each other accountable to the goals and directions they've established. The senior leadership encourages this process by defining the organization's overall direction and opportunity, then setting in place the standards or targets that each team will aim for within its authority, budget, and ministry parameters.

THE INTEGRATIVE PROCESS

Some congregations have large "silos" of ministry that aren't integrated with the rest of the congregation. In such cases, church members can't tell how all the ministries interconnect for their spiritual development, or how the ministries point in one direction (if they do). Churches need to address this with an integrative process.

The process requires teams to think interdependently. All members must value the ministries of other teams and seek to support their work. After all, each team has an overall goal related to the entire organization's vision. For churches, this might be stated as

To do God's will, or
To bring glory to God, or
To evangelize and make disciples.

Leaders integrate when they proceed with their work in a spirit of cooperation rather than competition. Most of this burden falls on the developmental coaches. They must link dispersed skills and competencies together into a coherent vision, and they must lend support and resources evenly across the ministries.

The integrating process also calls everyone to cooperate in sharing the precious resources of time, space, and money. This becomes a practical, day-to-day shift in perspective—many ministries constantly want the same time slots, seek a bigger piece of the budget, or try to schedule the same large room on any given evening.

Integrated understanding of the whole, with commitment to cooperation and interdependency, is what will maximize the work of all teams. For this to be done, the senior leadership must establish values and norms so everyone together can carry out effective problem-solving. Successes in these areas will show that an organizational culture of trust is blossoming.

THE RENEWAL PROCESS

In this new century, ministry, like business, faces enormous challenges. Powerful forces are at work against "the way we've always done it" in the church. These forces—within a culture that is quickly becoming apathetic to organized religion (but not to "spirituality")—threaten to marginalize or hinder once-thriving congregations.

Consider postmodernism, for example. Its assumptions about truth, and how it's best communicated, profoundly challenge the traditional church's methods. This is complicated by the rapid immigration that's making us an increasingly diverse, multicultural and multiethnic people; hence the undeniable need for an ongoing renewal process.

Frontline ministry teams must be continuously evaluating and adapting. Ongoing improvement is a must, and in this environment, change is the only true constant. Developmental coaches must balance between short-term performance ("How well are we ministering to existing audiences today?") and long-term impact ("How will we minister in the evolving picture in front of us?").

Part of the senior leadership's importance is keeping the organization's overarching purpose and mission the same while also regularly challenging long-standing assumptions and methods. At times they will need to experiment with new directions as they prepare for a different future.

To see these three processes in more concrete terms, take a look at the following three lists, which include the basics, in general categories, of the job descriptions for leadership's three rings. These represent what each ring is doing with its *entrepreneurial, integrating,* and *renewal* processes in ministries and organizations.

Ministry Teams (Frontline Entrepreneurs)

(1) *Take the part of the overall vision that is their responsibility and pursue opportunities to strategize for, and grow, ministries.*

(2) *Attract and develop laypeople, resources, gifts, and talents into competencies within these ministries and callings.*

(3) *Focus on building effectiveness of these parts of the organization's life (flywheel dynamics), developing the people (Q12 process), and building the teams and sub-teams.*

(4) *Innovate constantly, responding to new audiences (or changes in current audiences) to increase the ministry's breadth and depth.*

(5) *Respond to and be accountable for what the developmental coaches bring from other ministry teams and from the senior leadership.*

Developmental Coaches (Clergy and Layleaders)

(1) *Support and resource the ministry teams.*

(2) *Coordinate with other team leaders to:*
   (A) provide resources—money, space, people, and time—in critical venues;
   (B) link learning, skills, and "best practices" in other ministries for their particular team;
   (C) manage the tension of "our resource needs" between

their particular team and the other teams' needs;
(D) negotiate win/win dynamics among important cross-overs and boundaries with other teams.

(3) *Keep individual teams aware of the whole organization and where their particular ministry fits within it.*

(4) *Help interpret senior leadership's values, norms, and directions for individual teams.*

(5) *Report appropriate vision, measurements, performance, and successes to the senior leadership.*

Senior Leadership

(1) *Create an overarching organizational vision and purpose to set direction.*

(2) *Give clear span-of-care boundaries and responsibilities for each team, along with expectations and ways to stay accountable to senior leadership.*

(3) *Allow room for teams to stretch themselves into ever-widening impact, within the span-of-care guidelines and accountable relationships.*

(4) *Institute values and norms that build trust, cooperation, and support within and amongst the ministry teams.*

(5) *Challenge teams' assumptions at times, and help them stay accountable, focused on excellence and effectiveness.*

(6) *Have ongoing awareness of cultural dynamics:*
(A) within the organization—knowing what time it is for the organization;
(B) within the congregation—knowing "where we've been and where we're going";
(C) within the greater community.

(7) *When needed, redirect the church's resources in response to these changes in cultural context.*

Fleshing out these job descriptions for each team, coach, and senior leader will keep entrepreneurial, integrative, and renewal processes flowing in the organization's life. Doing so also means the processes will have a strong chance of staying effective over a long period of time. And that's exciting. These are the new wineskins from which the new wine can be poured! These help prevent the dangerous temptation to institutionalize our churches and ministries.

To sum up, consider Howard Snyder's take on the challenge:

Tradition can easily combine with the secular trends of modern society to produce an essentially institutional/organizational view of the church which clashes with the idea of the church as community and as a people. The modern technological revolution with it technocracy tends to reinforce the concept of the church-as-institution. This produces a concept of the church which is overly concerned with institutional and technical modes of operation and dangerously susceptible to management and behavioral techniques which owe more to B. F. Skinner than to Paul or Jesus. Significantly, Jesus rejected both religious and political hierarchical models for his followers.[4]

FOR THE GOOD OF THE WHOLE

We've already heard Christ's words about structure. Now let's return to the human body analogy and put these three processes in perspective. Our bodies constantly respond to new stimuli and new situations. We have well-developed sensory systems monitoring the environment to keep us informed, recommending and implementing adaptations in response. *Without* sensory systems, people suffer ill health and lack agility in an ever-changing world.

In other words, a body is constantly "innovating" throughout each day in order to thrive and grow. Additionally, if the human body lacked a well-integrated nervous system, merging all stimuli into a coherent whole, then chaos would ensue. Finally, without our brain's ability to learn, think, analyze, and grow, we couldn't respond to major changes in our climate or culture.

So far, we've explored a type of leadership that can handle the challenges of today and tomorrow. Yes, we face many fresh realities. And yes, these realities demand totally different structures and roles for both lay and professional leaders within churches. But the call to implement these structures is a good thing, a glorious thing. It tells us of our God, the one who keeps speaking into our hearts with an ever-fresh approach while still conveying the age-old gospel invitation to repentance and grace-filled living.

Jesus said to put "new wine into *new* wineskins." So consider: Are you ready to *create* the new wineskins needed to hold the new wine?"

FOR REFLECTION

Use this space to write down your reflections, reactions, insights, and responses to this chapter and its central question.

Am I ready to create the new wineskins needed to hold the new wine?

TEN

What Time Is It?

A young man trudged up the mountain toward a lone hermit living at the peak. The wise guru who would surely provide life's answers. At sundown, when the seeker finally reached the bleak little hut, he knocked and entered. "I've been expecting you," said the sage, with twinkling eyes. "You have come because of the great burden of your many problems."

"Yes," said the man, "and I will be so relieved if you'll help me solve them."

"The number of your problems," said the guru, "is greater, *by one,* than you think."

Despairing, the man asked, "What additional problem do I have?"

"You believe there will be a time when you will have no problems."

Ah! The flash of insight. Have you reached this enlightenment yet? As Jesus put it, "In this world you *will* have troubles."

No, the problems aren't going away, not in our personal lives and certainly not within our organizations, so the constant question for the leader is: "What particular set of problems am I facing at the moment?" Even new wine in new wineskins brings challenges (which we'll examine in the remaining chapters). The first challenge is to understand where, in its life cycle of development, your organization currently operates.

Ichak Adizes, author of *The Pursuit of Prime* and *Corporate Life-cycles,* has spent his entire career analyzing and describing this; he's a veritable life cycle guru, so listen closely to what he says about the challenge of keeping an organization moving toward *prime* functioning:

> *The key to success in management, then, is not to eliminate all problems, but to* focus on the problems of the present stage *of the organization's lifecycle so it can grow and mature to deal with the problems of the* next *stage. . . . To live means to continuously solve problems.*[1]

His point? Let's learn to *manage* the normal and healthy challenges and *eliminate* the destructive and unhealthy ones. To help managers understand this principle, Adizes uses the human life cycle as his developmental model.

At different stages (the inside of the curve on the diagram on next page), different types of leadership energy, or style, need to become dominant. This doesn't mean other leadership forms go away; however, certain types must take priority at certain stages if the organization is to thrive and develop. What are these types of energy? Consider the big four:

Entrepreneurial. This energy is creative and risk-taking, providing long-term vision so the organization can effectively accomplish its mission.

Performance. This energy manages the implementation of core purposes and services for short-term ministry effectiveness.

Administrative. This energy can systemize, routinize, and program a ministry's activities so the right things are done, at the right time, with the right intensity, allowing efficiency in day-to-day tasks.

Integrative. This energy can integrate all the functions into a culture of organic interdependence, allowing the organization to remain efficient over the long haul.

FIT YOUR LEADERSHIP TO LIFE CYCLES

Once we know these kinds of energies/styles, we can fit them into the life cycle stages leading up to "Prime" in Adizes' chart.[2] Here's how this might look.

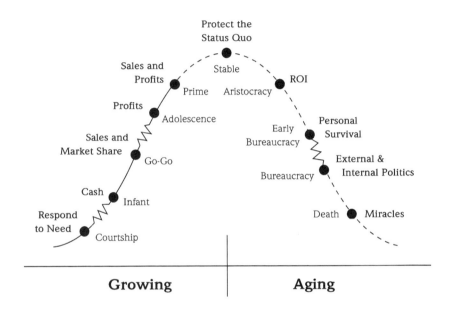

© Ichak Adizes: *Corporate Lifecycles* (Prentice Hall, 1989), p. 88.

THE COURTSHIP STAGE

In courtship, a church or ministry is just getting off the ground; this is where the enterprising leader, with entrepreneurial energy, works his magic. His gifts spur him to explain—clearly, powerfully—*why* this ministry has been created, then he inspires people with the vision. If this champion of the cause is able to recruit enough lay volunteers (or the church leadership is convinced that they should prioritize this ministry in the budget), the life cycle ascends to the next stage.

THE INFANCY STAGE

At this point, leadership energy switches from entrepreneurial to performing. The question of *why* transforms into *what*—what, exactly, are the tasks we need to be doing? And who is our "market" for this service or ministry? If we successfully attract people to involvement, we enter the next phase.

THE GO-GO STAGE

What an exciting time of ministry! Things are expanding rapidly. Once again, it's about performing—*additional* ministry to *greater* audiences with *more* people jumping on board. Meetings are lively, with all kinds of ideas and proposals bouncing off the walls. Not a lot of thought goes into organizing this exploding work God is doing; we're following as fast as He moves. But then, when a crises hits—maybe the money starts to fall short—the organization or ministry enters adolescence.

THE ADOLESCENT STAGE

Change is the watchword here. More is not better at this phase; *better* is better. Now administrative energy must come to the fore, and the word *no* emerges in planning meetings. The administrative leader raises questions of process, procedure, and efficiency because it's time to take the load off that single entrepreneur's shoulders— *time to have a group of people leading this ministry together.* Budgets are set and followed, and the ministry must now meet standards, being reviewed for impact related to resources. This is difficult but necessary; after all, if we want the ministry to sustain its next big growth spurt, systems must be in place. Further, with all efficient teams or departments functioning smoothly, the organization can enter its prime.

THE PRIME STAGE

Here's where a ministry can strategically plan its influence and impact, not just react to new opportunities, and the type of energy needed to do this is integrative. Integrative leaders help all the parts function as one unit, continually nurturing cross-functional planning to facilitate accomplishments that could never be done alone. All members also begin viewing the whole organization while continuing to passionately pursue their particular contributions. If this goes well, the organization, through planned strategy, will be able to open up more opportunities for ministry.

You may have noticed that imbedded in this discussion of stages are two important assumptions for us to embrace:

Assumption 1: Organizations have predictable stages and development points from which problems arise. *Each stage requires its own most-effective leadership energies to emerge* if growth is to continue.

Assumption 2: Leaders are usually wired for only one (perhaps two) of these styles; therefore, *they must know what time it is in the organization* in order to allow for different types of leaders to lead at the appropriate times.

A brief interlude into *LifeKeys,* with its exploration of personality types and gift identification, can help leaders ascertain their dominant leadership energy. To quickly summarize:

Enterprising Energy usually comes from having natural talents that are initiative and energetic in nature: persuading, negotiating, leading, speaking, selling, etc.

Performing Energy usually comes from both realistic natural talents and enterprising talents such as taking action, leading, managing, and exercising physical coordination.

Administrative Energy usually comes from conventional natural talents such as organizing, managing time, setting priorities, systematizing, and calculating. This can be backed up with investigative natural talents like researching, synthesizing, and conceptualizing.

Integrative Energy usually comes from social natural talents like expressing empathy, being tactful, listening and facilitating, teaching, understanding, and counseling.

KNOW THE TIMES

What are the implications of our discussion for most ministries and churches? A total shift in the understanding of leadership. Many currently view leadership as a gift (which it is); however, as we've seen, a church's leadership function, if it's to thrive over time, requires multiple gifts and multiple people at different moments in its life cycle. A familiar text conveys this sense of stages—or "seasons"—most wonderfully:

There is a time for everything,
*   and a season for every activity under heaven:*
a time to be born and a time to die,
*   a time to plant and a time to uproot,*
a time to kill and a time to heal,
*   a time to tear down and a time to build,*
a time to weep and a time to laugh,
*   a time to mourn and a time to dance,*
a time to scatter stones and a time to gather them,
*   a time to embrace and a time to refrain,*
a time to search and a time to give up,
*   a time to keep and a time to throw away,*
a time to tear and a time to mend,
*   a time to be silent and a time to speak,*
a time to love and a time to hate,
*   a time for war and a time for peace.*
ECCLESIASTES 3:1–8

Our individual lives proceed by seasons, and it's no different with groups. In terms of an organizational life cycle, there is clearly a time for a ministry to be born, a time for it to be planted, a time to build it up as large as possible. There is a time for its members to discern what to keep and what to throw, a time to uproot, and a time to refrain from certain activities, while embracing others. *Every activity has a season,* and, in terms of leaders, we might add:

so do they arrive at the times when they need to be the organization's central energy . . . and then the times when they should *not* be at the center.

I was excited when one of our executive presbyters asked me to consult with a church that needed help; the church's phone number indicated that it sat at the edge of an active city. I soon learned it had once been the town's center of action and that it had one of the most beautiful sanctuaries imaginable, with a one-thousand-seat capacity.

The problem? The congregation had dwindled to under one hundred active members.

As an entrepreneurial leader, I love entering this kind of situation; it requires a visionary style, exactly what I'm wired for. But wait! The interim pastor clearly was *not* wired like me, and even though he was leaving, he didn't want to rock the boat for these faithful hundred who were hanging on to their beautiful building (and barely paying for it with a quickly dwindling endowment). In my initial meeting with the layleaders, I immediately saw that my consulting potential had been sabotaged behind the scenes. No one wanted to ask, "What time is it for our church?" Consequently, the right type of leadership (which wasn't necessarily me) wasn't even being considered.

In contrast, when I flew in to consult with a congregation in another state, the senior pastor met me at the airport. He told me that the new pastor would soon arrive and how his own ministry was coming to a happy end. For the past fifteen years he'd been ministering in this downtown church, first embracing it when it was dying, then discerning (with the layleadership) exactly what the church's time was, back in those days. They began, piece by piece, to take care of the one hundred people who were left *and* to invest in appropriate changes to revitalize their ministries. Phase by phase, God gave them renewal. This church, years later, had become a national model of urban ministry.

Now one of my consulting goals was to help the members name "what time it was" in their church *today*. The senior pastor was willing to ask whether he was the right person for the *next* season of the church's growth. The difference? A leadership culture that kept asking, whatever might be the answer, "What time is it for us?" It was time to adapt to a new season. Everyone knew it, and the necessary transitions *could* unfold according to God's leading because its leaders were willing to lead as He intended.

LET THE LAY VOICES BE HEARD!

In my experience, layleadership often wishes to avoid the time question, yet they can't—they need to ask it, over and over, not abdicating responsibility to the pastor, lest they find themselves with pastors who have long overstayed their welcomes, the church going past its prime and aging toward expiration.

For an example of the *avoidance approach,* recall the days when ancient Israel cried out for a king. God never wanted the nation to have any ruler but Him, but He granted their demand because they wouldn't shoulder the responsibility of following Him—*that* took too much energy and commitment. Samuel, instructed by God, then proclaimed the consequent implications:

> When they said, "Give us a king to lead us," this displeased Samuel; so he prayed to the LORD. And the LORD told him: "Listen to all that the people are saying to you; it is not you they have rejected, but they have rejected me as their king. As they have done from the day I brought them up out of Egypt until this day, forsaking me and serving other gods, so they are doing to you. Now listen to them; but warn them solemnly and let them know what the king who will reign over them will do."
>
> Samuel told all the words of the LORD to the people who were asking him for a king. He said, "This is what the king who will reign over you will do: He will take your sons and make them serve with his chariots and horses, and they will

*run in front of his chariots. Some he will assign to be com-
manders of thousands and commanders of fifties, and others to
plow his ground and reap his harvest, and still others to make
weapons of war and equipment for his chariots. He will take
your daughters to be perfumers and cooks and bakers. He will
take the best of your fields and vineyards and olive groves and
give them to his attendants. He will take a tenth of your grain
and of your vintage and give it to his officials and attendants.
Your menservants and maidservants and the best of your cattle
and donkeys he will take for his own use. He will take a tenth
of your flocks, and you yourselves will become his slaves. When
that day comes, you will cry out for relief from the king you
have chosen, and the* LORD *will not answer you in that day."*

*But the people refused to listen to Samuel. "No!" they said.
"We want a king over us. Then we will be like all the other
nations, with a king to lead us and to go out before us and fight
our battles."*

1 SAMUEL 8:6–20

Samuel clearly describes what a human king will bring to them
and take from them. Even when the people pray, God won't deliver
them; *they have abdicated responsibility for their organization
(nation).* Their response is revealing:

- We want to look like other nations.

- We want someone else to lead and make decisions for us.

- We want someone else to fight our battles.

I often see such abdication in churches when layleaders give
their authority over to pastors. In the name of either looking like
other churches or wanting others to make choices for them, they
give away their freedom to ask, "What time is it here?" Then, when
they need a new type of leadership to take the church to its next
stage of the life cycle, there are no layleader voices to make sure it
actually happens.

In Adizes' model, the difficulty that authority figures have in recognizing the need for different leadership is called the "Founder's Trap." What was necessary to get the vision and direction started—or even to develop it through the Go-Go phase—could be exactly what will hinder the organization as it approaches adolescence or heads toward prime.

Consider instead the *assertive approach*. Remember the council of Jerusalem in Acts? The early church faced a crossroads: Would it require new Gentile believers to submit to all the regulations of the Judaism from which it emerged? Would the keeping of Hebrew law be a requirement for church membership?

The council called together many church leaders to work on this issue, keeping multiple voices in the discussion as they sought God's guidance. And what happened? I love the line in the letter they wrote to the churches: "It seemed good to the Holy Spirit and to us . . ." (15:28). This was a group of Christian leaders working together to discern God's will. They refused to give over their voices to a single leader who would make their decisions for them.

Let's apply these insights by looking at the development of an adult educational ministry in a church I consulted. When new leadership took over this ministry, it was one of the congregation's least developed (children's and youth ministries had dominated the church's life for years). The new visionary leader, bursting with enterprising energy, felt that if the small-group and classroom ministries were combined into one spiritual formation team, and if the focus was on developing both small groups and lay teachers, the adult education ministry would expand. He maintained that if the children and youth were going to have models of long-term church involvement, then the adults needed to be growing in their faith.

As people began responding to the call, a ministry team and paid staff came together. Training was extended to the team members, the small-group leaders, and the classroom teachers. Trial-

and-error experimenting occurred on various evenings and Sunday mornings. As the team got better and better at recruiting, training, publicizing, and supporting teachers and small-group leaders, the Go-Go phase set in. The ministry expanded in many directions— men's, women's, and couples groups flourished.

After years of expansion, a need for new leadership energy became apparent. The ministry needed more structure, so the church called a new small-group director. Expansion had also brought diversity, which required that the ministry team and elected leaders work on a theological statement that set clear ministerial direction and boundaries.

Furthermore, these ministries needed accurate reporting and evaluation, so the leadership took on the arduous task of computerizing growth, year to year, and incorporating standard reporting procedures. All of this was tapping into the administrative energy needed to put the ministry on a firmer foundation going into the future.

As the ministry came out of adolescence and began to move toward prime, both enterprising and integrative energy emerged front and center. Rather than simply reacting to the opportunities before them, the team strategically developed a way to disciple laypeople by creating, testing, and building a mentoring ministry. The congregation's senior leadership also made a significant change in creating a Gen-X worship service and then discerning how to build an educational ministry to service this audience. One conclusion: We need once again to change adult ministry leaders!

The original visionary was a Baby Boomer; it was time to call a person within the age range of the audience the congregation now wanted to connect with: Gen-X. At this writing, the leadership of the Gen-X service and the new adult-ed leader are working out a strategy to integrate these ministries.

We can see this unveiling of stages when we look at human growth. Early in a child's development come basic speech patterns. Then refined motor skills such as walking, running, and climbing take the stage. When a child heads off to school, cognitive thinking becomes the big development issue. Eventually, sexuality and differentiation into a unique personality become the major work.

My point: The body's endocrine system uses *different* hormones—with a right time and stage for every phase—to regulate growth from childhood into full development. So it is with our organizations: By embracing life cycles we can use the most effective leadership at the right times. By staying alert we can keep asking the question that will help us always be ready for the new, the exciting, the fresh. Isn't this the very definition of God's ever-expanding kingdom among us?

FOR REFLECTION

Use this space to write down your reflections, reactions, insights, and responses to this chapter and its central question.

What time is it in our organizational life cycle?

ELEVEN

Are You Trying to Fill a Niche or Simply Expand as Far as Possible?

When organizations begin using the leadership principles we've been exploring, they usually experience some immediate successes. The excitement builds, they often enter the Go-Go phase, and that's when a great temptation frequently rears its ugly head: *Let's expand just as far as we can go!*

Wouldn't it be better for the group to discern its niche within the overall scheme of God's plans? In *What We Learned in the Rainforest,* Mitsubishi Electric CEO Tachi Kiuchi and environmental advocate Bill Shireman describe the dilemma[1] by comparing two different types of organizational growth to rainforest plants.

The first type is *mangrove growth.* Mangroves get a singular foothold next to salt water, surviving the brine because their roots filter much of the salt and because their enzyme systems secrete the rest while storing fresh water. They also employ an aerial root system that "snorkels" for air above oxygen-poor mud; on their surface, these roots utilize special pores called lenticels, through which only air (not water or salts) can pass.

With such marvelous advantages, mangroves dominate any other plant species growing near salt water; nevertheless, they eventually engineer their own demise by expanding rapidly with no sense of the change they are causing in their environment. Sooner or later the very conditions that help mangroves flourish become their worst poison, and other species then take over where they once thrived. Here's what happens:

> *One very important environmental service produced by the mangroves is that they also build land or keep it from being washed away. Mud and sediment are often washed down rivers and streams. When there is a mangrove swamp at the river mouth, the water spreads out into the mangroves, and the sediment settles to the bottom where it is trapped by the mangrove roots. As the bottom gets shallower, the mangroves can grow further out, while those on the inside eventually find themselves on dry land, where they are replaced by land plants. In this way the mangrove forest advances slowly outward, leaving land behind.*[2]

Regarding the mangrove phenomenon, I know of one visionary church planter who diligently researched a rapidly growing part of town. His small group acquired a large piece of land, and the church seemed off to a good start: Soon they were growing, with a huge expansion of buildings, a diverse set of ministries, and numerous outreach endeavors expanding in all directions.

They were known for "doing many things," regardless of context or forethought. The excitement lasted for a time, but the axiom "If you build it, they will come" didn't hold true; as mortgage obligations escalated, leaders had to start selling off assets simply to make payments. Staff layoffs came next, and disillusionment set in. As I write, I wonder whether the congregation will still exist in three to five years.

The second type of organizational increase might be called *typical rainforest growth.* Though a foliage canopy blocks most of the light and uses up much rain, the rainforest practices amazing conservation of resources. Every plant has a niche and a specific purpose to fulfill within this burgeoning ecosystem; plants weave together to create a complex, coordinated structure in which very little is wasted. Every possible space supports some form of life.

The big idea for leadership here is to know and make the most of rainforest growth distinctives. *Each species plays the role it's designed to play and fills its niche.* Each species also seems to know its limits and boundaries amidst the cooperative/competitive relationship with all others surrounding it; the rainforest doesn't die off through uncontrolled, non-conserving expansion, but instead continues in equilibrium.

I know of one successful congregation that clearly knew its limitations and the specific contributions it could make to its community. After growing to a certain point, the senior pastor realized the church's property wouldn't hold another large building; he also felt a better use of the congregation's competencies— and land, money, and time—would be to spin off other churches in the area. After a decade of planting, the original church members now enjoy the warm glow of seeing many thriving congregations that are, in effect, their spiritual children and grandchildren.

That church *also* continues to grow at a steady rate. Such churches and organizations will be thriving long into the future, even lasting for multiple generations, if they continue to follow rainforest wisdom. Paul followed this path in his own ministry, which he addresses while speaking to certain boastful leaders:

We do not dare to classify or compare ourselves with some who commend themselves. When they measure themselves by themselves and compare themselves with themselves, they are not wise.

We, however, will not boast beyond proper limits, but will confine our boasting to the field God has assigned to us, a field that reaches even to you. We are not going too far in our boasting, as would be the case if we had not come to you, for we did get as far as you with the gospel of Christ. Neither do we go beyond our limits by boasting of work done by others.

Our hope is that, as your faith continues to grow, our area of activity among you will greatly expand, so that we can preach the gospel in the regions beyond you. For we do not want to boast about work already done in another man's territory. But, "Let him who boasts boast in the Lord." For it is not the one who commends himself who is approved, but the one whom the Lord commends.

2 CORINTHIANS 10:12–18

Paul teaches that God assigns different fields or spheres of influence to every ministry. Accordingly, he limited his work to the field God assigned him, refusing to claim credit for work done in another person's territory.

This radical path to organizational expansion is becoming a common way of viewing how organizations ought to operate, and James F. Moore, in *The Death of Competition,* argues for its prevalence in today's business climate. Companies traditionally thought about simply improving their products and services relative to their competition, believing that if they could offer a better mousetrap, they'd gain the larger market share.

"Not so!" says Moore—life isn't nearly so basic these days. Many mega-companies can now enter and capture a whole industry virtually overnight. While you're trying to make your mousetrap marginally better, MouseBeGone, Inc., has suddenly discovered how to fill every house with a rodent-repellant sound, undetectable to the human ear, through a device available in supermarkets for only $3.95. A brand-new way of meeting an age-old need may have just run you out of the mouse business.

Mere product- and service-improvement won't thrive in today's business world. The alternative is to look at the whole ecosystem of interaction in your particular arenas, then either find an existing niche/role or create a new one that evolves as the overall marketplace changes. Moore puts it like this:

The new paradigm requires thinking in terms of whole systems—that is, seeing your business as part of a wider economic ecosystem and environment. Systems thinking is a mental capability that can be strengthened and improved. The basic idea is simple. Understand the economic systems evolving around you and find ways to contribute. Start with an understanding of the big picture rather than of products and services.[3]

Does Moore's thesis apply to church life as well as to organizational life? Over the past few decades, the American church has heard from a few market research "prophets" who keep us all aware of how drastically the secular culture's ecosystem is changing in its attitudes toward faith. Let's take a quick glimpse into the work of just two, George Barna and Robert Wuthnow. In *Grow Your Church From the Outside In,* Barna shows what's been happening, by generation, to church attendance.

- Ages 65+   23% don't attend

- Ages 50–64   29% don't attend

- Ages 35–49   33% don't attend

- Ages 25–34   36% don't attend

- Ages 18–24   46% don't attend[4]

In light of this steady decline, Barna, asking us to consider how we might attract and bring back many of the non-churched, summarizes his overall thinking this way:

To make the most of existing opportunities, and to create additional ones, we need to recognize that the unchurched market is divided into self-defined niches. The people within each of these niches have different degrees of likelihood of joining the church.[5]

Barna and Moore both suggest that we'll need to thoroughly understand our culture, viewing the whole horizon of communities around our church and starting to find ways to contribute to them through creative means that attract their various niche groups. If this seems new and radical, realize that Paul was utilizing similar strategy long ago.

> *Though I am free and belong to no man, I make myself a slave to everyone, to win as many as possible. To the Jews I became like a Jew, to win the Jews. To those under the law I became like one under the law (though I myself am not under the law), so as to win those under the law. To those not having the law I became like one not having the law (though I am not free from God's law but am under Christ's law), so as to win those not having the law. To the weak I became weak, to win the weak. I have become all things to all men so that by all possible means I might save some. I do all this for the sake of the gospel, that I may share in its blessings.*
> 1 CORINTHIANS 9:19–23

Paul analyzed any audience he was seeking to win to Christ, and he adjusted his "way of being" to influence the particular group he served. How can it be good strategy for churches in a growth phase to act like mangroves, attempting to expand in all directions? It doesn't seem to be the apostolic way—and it might even be a formula for quick decline! Paul's approach calls for a group of leaders to monitor their environment and keep leading their organization in forms of ministry experimentation, that is, constantly trying out ways to contribute.

By the way, both Bill Hybels at Willow Creek and Rick Warren at Saddleback did this when they built their successful ministries. Neither was trying to do incrementally better in the same old manner; both analyzed their communities and tailored their ministries to respond to the niche marketplaces they found around them.

Before we look at some of the best thinking about the essence of such visioning and strategic planning, let me stress once again:

Our situation in the church is becoming critical. In his outstanding book *After Heaven: Spirituality in America Since the 1950s,* Dr. Robert Wuthnow, a well-known and widely published sociology professor, asks, "Why aren't people attending church today?"

His answer: People have changed! While they were once *joiners,* now they're *questers* on a journey. As noted earlier, they've also become enamored with the difference between spirituality and institutional religion. ("I'm not religious, but I *am* spiritual" has become a postmodern mantra.) "Religion" is only one source of spiritual inspiration; spirituality is now broadly defined as "making meaning, finding connection, and gaining purpose through drawing inspiration from many sources." Wuthnow's statistics for the year 2000 offer confirmation:

- 9 out of 10 people thought it was possible to be a good Christian or Jew without attending any worship services;

- 8 out of 10 thought an individual should arrive at his own beliefs, independent of any religious organization;

- 7 out of 10 thought all religions are equally good at finding ultimate truth.[6]

For church leaders, these attitudes signal the scale of the evangelistic challenge ahead. In the language of our current discussion, why focus on competing with any other church? We need to keep our attention fixed on the massive cultural shift rocking our world, and we must keep asking, "How might we respond to the new niches of people in our community?" As we answer, we'll be ready and willing to change whatever is not core so we can address our actual spiritual environment . . . and thrive over the coming decades.

STAGE ONE: KNOW YOUR CORE, THEN EXPERIMENT

With this background firmly in mind, let's look at some of the important ideas from business that I'm convinced can help the church respond to our ever-changing environment.

At this point I'm assuming that your church (or organization) has already developed a mission statement and clearly defined its purposes and values, that you've envisioned your future and developed goals that are moving you in the right direction. What happens next, however, as your organization begins to grow, is our question at hand: How do we expand our growth in strategic ways? We know we want to avoid mangrove death, but what do we actually *do*?

According to Moore, as you enter the first stage of interacting with the environment, you walk into the Terrain of Opportunities. Here the church or organization begins to experiment—by action, feedback, and reflection—with new ways of doing ministry and mission within the community. The key point to remember: Most new opportunities will build upon already-existing core competencies, *not* trying to create nonexisting competencies.

This is the primary insight of Chris Zook and James Allen in *Profit From the Core* and *Beyond the Core*. A brief review of the *Profit From the Core* theme:

> *In this short, focused, and well-reasoned book, Zook, the head of worldwide strategy for the prestigious consulting and investment firm Bain & Co., and Allen, head of a venture-capital company, argue persuasively that* focusing on what a business does best *is the easiest and most efficient way for companies to grow and be profitable. This idea isn't new, of course: In the 1980s, Tom Peters and Robert Waterman, in their classic* In Search of Excellence, *called it "sticking to your knitting"; a decade later, most notably in the Harvard Business Review, Gary Hamel and C. K. Prahalad described the concept as focusing on "core competencies." But, Zook and Allen maintain, as firms rushed to embrace the Internet, executives forgot this basic truth. Taking the idea one step further, they contend that by looking at what a firm does best, executives will also find it easy to spot inefficiencies within their businesses. Based on a study of*

*2,000 companies, the book concludes that three factors differen-
tiate growth strategies that work from those that don't:
(1) make sure to get everything possible out of the core business,
(2) expand into related businesses and (3) redefine the business
before someone else (e.g., a competitor) does.[7]*

The diagram[8] below lends visual power to these emphases,
showing the lack of success businesses experience when they try to
expand beyond their existing core competency.

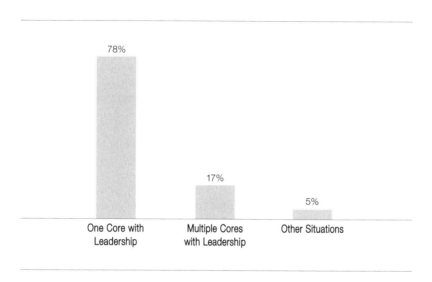

Profit From the Core, Chris Zook with James Allen; copyright © 2001 Bain &
Company, Inc. Reprinted with permission of Harvard Business School Press.

As you can see, only 17 percent of companies could create sus-
tained value that went beyond their original core set of talents. My
conclusion? Start your ministry experiments with the talents, passions, and competencies your organization already has. Once again,
the Bain research helps us with a diagram[9] of adjacent possibilities
that companies use when expanding to possible markets for their
products and services.

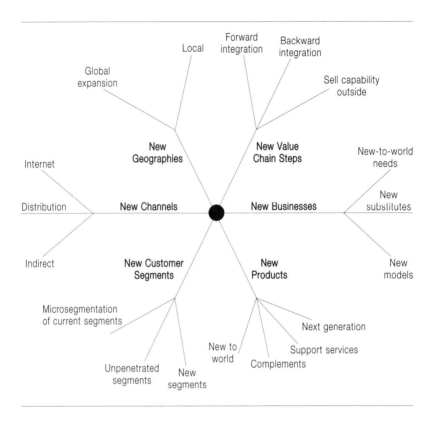

Profit From the Core, Chris Zook with James Allen; copyright © 2001 Bain & Company, Inc. Reprinted with permission of Harvard Business School Press.

Ready to think about how these ideas could work for a local church?

Leadership begins by establishing processes to identify and clarify the passions, talents, and competencies already existing in the congregational life, inviting everyone to keep asking: "What do we do best around here?" Some churches may stand out through meaningful, powerful worship experiences; others may excel at teaching the Bible; still others may do a wonderful job at gathering people into caring small groups. In any case, they keep asking and answering: "What is the one thing (or few things) of excellence that characterizes our life together—the thing we can also offer to others?"

The answers do not need to be highly developed before experimentation can begin . . . in ways, for example, like the following.

(1) TRY ADDING SUPPORTIVE MINISTRIES

Add supportive ministries to each of your existing core ministry competencies; in this way you immediately expand these ministries' capacities and impact. In some cases, you'll be thinking in terms of the next generation: "What can we add to reach *these* (new) folks with what we're already doing well for *those* folks?" For example, many churches moved away from offering just one traditional worship service to also offering a contemporary service. Today, some are moving from contemporary to postmodern (or emerging) worship. *It's all about continuing the same mission and values, but adding very different tactics and processes to deliver the same ministry.*

(2) TRY REACHING NEW GEOGRAPHIES AND/OR AUDIENCES

You'll find expansion opportunities within a certain radius of your church. The leadership could study at least three potential audiences that might be places of growth, then consider: "Which of these audiences have the best possible match with the audience already attending here?" For instance, they might be: people who visit; people in relationship with active members; people living within the church's perimeter (usually a five- or ten-mile radius). Experiments could involve adjusting current ministries to attract or involve these new audiences.

(3) TRY UPDATING AND EXPANDING MODES OF COMMUNICATION

Sometimes the way to experiment with increasing a congregation's impact isn't about new audiences or services. Instead, members can consider: "How are we communicating to the world at large?" That is, "why not update and expand the way we make ourselves known?" This can be a great way to communicate with people otherwise unaware of your ministry. Many thriving churches are incorporating new communication media, including Web sites, video screens, and e-mail newsletters—simple ways to expand the "distribution network," bringing awareness to people who potentially would become involved with your congregation.

(4) TRY REDECORATING THE "FRONT DOOR" FOR NON-ATTENDERS

For many, a Sunday morning worship service for believers is not going to work as a first step into your church fellowship. As we've seen, people today may be spiritually hungry while not believing they need to attend a church to build their faith; in response, churches can experiment with ways to better interface with them. "Do we need a seeker-targeted service? Do we need to expand our small-group ministries to include spiritual questers? Do we need to focus on acts of kindness done in the community?" Any of these questions can lead to experimental ministries to repaint your church's front door in an inviting color. Seekers can have an entrance that says "welcome" in their language.

(5) TRY MAKING USE OF OUTSIDE MARKET RESEARCH

There's a wealth of resource information to help you understand your community and identify possible exploratory niches for your church. Some research builds on existing church demographics. Other studies include specifically contracted surveys reporting on the direction of the culture at large. These are invaluable in helping senior leaders shape their thinking as they work to understand the unchurched around them. Here's an example of the information and insight that the Barna group (for instance) can provide:

> *Consistent with other findings from our research, we discovered that of the seven descriptions tested, the approach that appeals the most to the unchurched is an active involvement in helping poor and disadvantaged people. Half of the unchurched said*

*that this type of positioning makes a church "very appealing,"
and another one-third said it makes a church "somewhat
appealing." This image is especially appealing to women,
downscale individuals and black adults.*

*The next most attractive positioning is to communicate that
the church is meeting the needs of the entire family unit. About
two out of five adults said this makes a church "very appealing," and one-third said it makes the church "somewhat
appealing." Nearly identical results were obtained when we
asked about positioning a church as concerned about the declin-
ing morals in American society.*

*Being known as a place that helps people apply Christianity
to their daily lives was slightly less appealing to people, but it
still drew positive reaction from a majority. Lesser appeal was
associated with being positioned as a church that is "relevant
for your life today" or being "biblically based." By far the least
appealing image was being a church that is politically active.
Only 1 out of 10 adults said that such an image made the
church "very appealing," and 2 out of 10 stated that such a
church would be "somewhat appealing" to them. Most significantly, half of the unchurched said that a church that prides
itself on being politically active would be "not at all appealing"
to them.*[10]

However an organization chooses to experiment within its
unique Terrain of Opportunities, it needs to be intentional about
trial, feedback, and systemized learning within the process. Constantly ask about effectiveness and then use your findings to make
adjustments for a better approach to potential audiences. In *What
We Learned in the Rainforest,* Kiuchi and Shireman diagram[11] this
with a series of steps that occur in ecosystems as organisms establish an environmental niche.

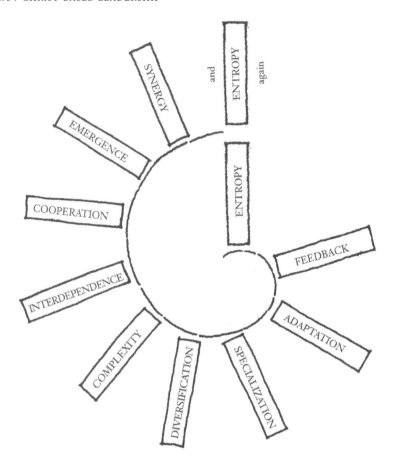

Let's think about how a congregation might use these steps to strategically expand its community impact.

First, it experiments amidst its *entropy* (that is, in the midst of change, unpredictability, and potential energy).

It gathers *feedback,* from which it makes adjustments and implements *adaptation,* allowing it to continue experimentation with new ministries.

After many trials, this begins to create a *specialization* for the congregation around one of its core competencies.

This specialization causes the new ministry to *diversify* into new audiences.

As people use their gifts and talents around this direction, it grows into the *complexity* of a series of interconnected ministries offered in the new niche.

Soon these ministries become *interdependent* and are working in *cooperation* with other ministries or outside organizations.

Thus they find *emergence* into a more permanent place within the communities they are serving, continuing in an effective *synergy*.

Until . . .

Until *entropy* takes over again—the new cultural shift, the new societal change, the new and unpredictable potential for growth. The experimentation continues . . . getting feedback . . . adjusting ministry . . . and on and on and on.

One church I know started experimenting with what it called Gen-X worship. The ministry group surrounded the sanctuary with a black curtain, held services in the evenings, and created a worship atmosphere that included candles, rock instruments, interactive preaching, and a post-service gathering around refreshments.

As the Gen-X group rapidly expanded, it added concerts once a month, which in turn expanded the audience even more dramatically. To maintain and increase awareness, the group used posters, Web sites, and other media-savvy vehicles that were familiar. Talented individuals worked on numerous teams dedicated to each ministry phase. Today, this once fledgling group is an entire church community with many interdependencies of service and ministry all coalesced around their worship style.

What begins to emerge from this Terrain of Opportunities process is thrilling—whole new ways of going about ministry and mission for existing churches. Every congregation should have at least some part of its ministry dedicated to this process. Furthermore, the experiments are strategic, having some sense of the match between the competencies of the existing organization and the right fit within the community around the church.

Sometimes a new sense of identity emerges from the directions being pursued. A biblical example comes from Acts 13, where church leaders discerned that Paul and Barnabas ought to be set aside for a new work. They received heartfelt prayer and then launched into their missionary journeys, on which Paul's usual method was to enter synagogues and preach the message of Jesus. Typically, some or many Jews would convert and begin churches in these locations.

As Paul kept encountering resistance from synagogue leaders, suffering greatly as a result, God had other plans for him and led him to focus on a different audience from city to city. He began preaching to the—hold on, this is radical!—to the . . . Gentiles. With magnificent success.

As Paul reflected on this "experiment," God gave him a text from the Old Testament to confirm this call on his life: "I have made you a light for the Gentiles, that you may bring salvation to the ends of the earth" (v. 47; see Isaiah 49:6). More and more, as God directed, we see Paul focusing his established competencies of evangelism and discipleship on the Gentile population. (He mentions in Galatians how God had been speaking to him about this specific call, confirmed in action as he trekked through the nations.)

Like Paul, churches and organizations will be given specific spheres of influence from which they are to do their work. In this first stage of experimentation, congregations often discover their special "field," along with the directions attached to it. They must decide whether they will risk moving forward by faith.

STAGE TWO: SPREAD THE REVOLUTION AND EXPAND

Moving forward in a changing environment eventually brings us to Stage Two, which James Moore describes as Spreading the Revolution. The goal is to expand the experimentation to the point that it scales up to a significant size. This can be more difficult than

Stage One, because the challenges are not external but internal.

During Stage Two, many of the biggest challenges are at the process, organizational, and stakeholder levels. Scaling and replication require well-designed, standard processes. These in turn depend upon well-managed organizations. Taking an organization through aggressive growth requires risk capital, which must be provided by stakeholders.[12]

Some church members may feel threatened at this stage. They might think, for example, "Hey, I've been doing this ministry for a long time. Now all these new groups have started—and they're using money from the budget that *we've* been funding for years. Something's wrong with this picture!"

Such natural reactions will test leadership's wisdom and conflict-resolution skills. They must be able to connect the "old" and the "expanded" by way of the whole congregation's core mission and values. With excellent communication and interpersonal skills these leaders can help longtime members see a logical connection between the history of the church and the new ways of doing mission and ministry. Thus members will recognize continuity while seeing that tactical and operational changes were necessary. "After all," they'll eventually say, "how else could our church keep going in this developing world?" (By the way, at least 20 percent of the established leadership must get behind a new direction in order to avoid killing off the emerging life.)

Obviously, many of us will need to refine a whole new set of leadership skills. Throughout much of the twentieth century, the institutional church enjoyed a monopoly in America; there weren't many alternatives for those in search of "a spirituality." No more! Now leaders must take at least three steps:

(1) *Develop your ability to discern new directions for your congregation so it can effectively respond to the changing cultural environment.*

(2) *Make sure your congregation is constantly experimenting in ministry and then analyzing feedback so it can continually adapt and thrive.*

(3) *Establish within your congregation a culture that both celebrates the old and welcomes the new, all under the common and unchanging goals, values, and competencies.*

Once again, we can look to the human body as an example. Over the life-span certain schemas (or "pathways") form in the brain, telling a person "how I will be" in the world. These patterns are essential to the formation of a stable personality. However, the older a person becomes, the more difficult for him or her to see other legitimate but *different* ways of being.

What can help a person broaden? One specific boost can come from connecting the "new way of being" with what is already familiar behavior (with some adjustments). Such connection and expansion is vital to creating long-term change. Really, isn't this the only way to keep growing and learning as a human being, throughout our lives? We experiment with new behavior, and, through our sensory and memory systems, we learn new ways of being in the world.

We return to some key questions, however, that will arise as congregations expand and grow. Is our focus purely internal? Are we simply trying to expand as much as possible? Or could we move our focus over to the external environment and try finding the best place for our competencies to develop and contribute to this ever-changing community? Given our culture's drastic spiritual shifts, our responses could mean the difference between mangrove-like decay and luxuriant rainforest abundance.

FOR REFLECTION

Use this space to write down your reflections, reactions, insights, and responses to this chapter and its central question.

Am I trying to fill a niche or simply expand as far as possible?

TWELVE

Who Are You Here to Serve?

Here's where we've traveled in our leadership explorations:

Way back in chapter 1, we began by asking, "What is the truth of your ambition?" and found that Level 5 leaders can achieve a balance between humility and drive. This humility, according to chapter 2, allows us to bow to the Lord of our leadership, Jesus Christ, and respond to His guidance in *all* aspects of our lives.

Our faith must also extend to the flawed people (folks just like us!) whom we're leading, as we saw in chapter 3. We can believe in those people—we can believe they'll do the right thing with excellence—if only we'll give them the chance. This moves us to nurture an entire culture based on trust and accountability rather than fear and compliance, an environment in which we obtain the freedom to embrace a whole new definition of success (explained in chapter 4): Equipping others to minister means our own success can only mean the success of *everyone* in the group.

This definition refocuses our attention; as we saw in chapter 5, we begin looking beyond the few strong performers to attend to ministry teams or task forces where people work together in effective synergy. Team leaders, in turn, take up the challenge of putting people in the right positions and developing them over time, endeavoring to build dynamic cohesiveness and inviting people to transcend their own personal agendas in favor of the team goals.

Still with me? If so, you know we've now reached the concepts of chapter 6, where we noted that all this team effort can thrive in a culture more committed to *excellence* than winning; a flywheel culture (utilizing step-by-step transformation) rather than a doom loop culture (lurching into radical change efforts). The result of all this equipping, developing, and playing to strengths (chapter 7) is a highly beneficial cooperation (chapter 8) that will cause the structures—the new wineskins!—of our organizations to become less hierarchical, more organic. According to chapter 9, an organic organization builds upon three different leadership roles: frontline entrepreneurs, developmental coaches, and institutional builders. Each has a unique role in the three central processes—entrepreneurial, integrative, and renewing.

In chapter 10 we asked, "What time is it?" If you answered, "I know what time it is in the life cycle of my organization," then please stay on the line for a description of your prize. In chapter 11 you considered whether you'll spend the rest of your ministry days expanding wildly into a muddy delta so you can suffer a slow and painful death . . . or . . . trek into the verdant rainforest of healthy organizational growth (via niches and competencies).

If you've been able to recall and retain these key concepts, I applaud you. If you've mastered them and even begun applying them in your organization, I laud you. If you've gathered people around you and begun studying diligently with the goal of beginning a process of organizational transformation that will bring you health and growth over the long haul, I enthusiastically extol your diligence and drive, and I pray for God's blessing upon you as you move forward.

In any case, for sticking with me through this whirlwind review of our journey, let me be the first to welcome you to chapter 12.

NEEDED: NEW PRINCIPLES, NEW CONTRACT

Peter Block, in *Stewardship: Choosing Service Over Self-Interest*, suggests that organic leadership not only requires a new set of *principles* but also a completely different *contract* between leaders and followers. Before we look at the principles and the contract, listen to Block's words regarding this:

> *Stewardship holds the possibility of shifting our expectations of people in power. Part of the meaning of stewardship is to hold in trust the well-being of some larger entity—our organization, our community, and the earth itself. To hold something of value in trust calls for placing service ahead of control, to no longer expect leaders to be in charge and out front. There is pride in leadership, it evokes images of direction. There is humility in stewardship, it evokes images of service.*[1]

Why *stewardship*? When Block uses the term as his master image for leadership, he actually echoes Jesus. In fact, most of Jesus' teachings on leadership come to us through the "stewardship parables," a rich portion of the gospel tradition. Read this one carefully.

> *[Jesus said,] "Be dressed ready for service and keep your lamps burning, like men waiting for their master to return from a wedding banquet, so that when he comes and knocks they can immediately open the door for him. It will be good for those servants whose master finds them watching when he comes. I tell you the truth, he will dress himself to serve, will have them recline at the table and will come and wait on them. It will be good for those servants whose master finds them ready, even if he comes in the second or third watch of the night. But understand this: If the owner of the house had known at what hour the thief was coming, he would not have let his house be broken into. You also must be ready, because the Son of Man will come at an hour when you do not expect him."*
>
> *Peter asked, "Lord, are you telling this parable to us, or to everyone?"*
>
> *The Lord answered, "Who then is the faithful and wise*

manager, whom the master puts in charge of his servants to give them their food allowance at the proper time? It will be good for that servant whom the master finds doing so when he returns. I tell you the truth, he will put him in charge of all his possessions. But suppose the servant says to himself, 'My master is taking a long time in coming,' and he then begins to beat the menservants and maidservants and to eat and drink and get drunk. The master of that servant will come on a day when he does not expect him and at an hour he is not aware of. He will cut him to pieces and assign him a place with the unbelievers.

"That servant who knows his master's will and does not get ready or does not do what his master wants will be beaten with many blows. But the one who does not know and does things deserving punishment will be beaten with few blows. From everyone who has been given much, much will be demanded; and from the one who has been entrusted with much, much more will be asked."

LUKE 12:35–48

In other parables also, *Jesus frames all work and leadership through the lens of stewardship.* God is like a landlord who has gone away on a journey, trusting his servants to do their assignments until he returns. The point is that Christian faithfulness means responding to the task we've been given. Notice that faithful stewards

- dress themselves to be ready for service;

- watch for the Master's return;

- give resources at the proper time to others;

- obey the Master's will;

- know that when much has been given, much is required.

Jesus paints the opposite picture of those who don't embrace their stewardship. These folks are

- not ready for service, partying and distracted;

- not watching for the Master's return;

- not treating others with respect;

- not disciplined, doing whatever they want;

- not doing what's required of their giftedness.

Stewardship means being willing to shoulder God's trust that we'll accomplish our assigned tasks until Jesus comes again. Block argues that our organizations need just this type of responsibility in their leaders.

> *Stewardship is the set of principles and practices which have the potential to make dramatic changes in our governance system. It is concerned with creating a way of governing ourselves that creates a strong sense of ownership and responsibility for outcomes at the bottom line. . . . It means creating self reliance on the part of all who are touched by the institution.*[2]

Imagine that, Mr. and Ms. Leader. Creating a sense of responsibility for outcomes . . . *at the bottom!* Talk about relieving stress—wouldn't that be great? Good stewardship makes it happen.

NOW, ABOUT THOSE PRINCIPLES . . .

Keeping our theme in mind, let's move ahead with Block as he outlines leadership principles that create this sense of stewardship in leaders and in organizations. In each case, I'll try to relate the principle to a concept we've covered in our previous chapters.[3]

MAXIMIZE CHOICES FOR THOSE CLOSEST TO THE WORK

This first principle came out in our discussions of the need for new structure. The front lines are wherever teams are doing the visioning and ministry. They're closest to the actual work; therefore, they need to have the information, resources, and support to make the best decisions for their roles. Good stewarding leadership trusts these folks to know what's best (since they're the experts at their particular function) and allows them broad decision-making discretion. Mistake-tolerance may also apply to this area.

REINTEGRATE "MANAGING" WITH "DOING THE WORK"

This principle tells us why so much of the work usually assigned to senior leadership is now given back to developmental coaches and ministry teams. Senior leaders have a unique role, but their work docs *not* involve controlling and monitoring teams' day-to-day activities. Teams receive targets and expectations, then they move ahead with all freedom to accomplish these objectives however they choose to do them. Good stewardship leaders can handle that.

GIVE A BASIC STRUCTURE, THEN SUPPORT SELF-DIRECTION

A close cousin to the previous principle, this one arose in many of our discussions related to team-based work. Senior leadership communicates vision and reinforces organizational values, then teams are allowed to build synergy in the context of providing continuous feedback. That is, they're constantly saying: "Here's where we are with goals; here's what we need in coaching; here's how we want to connect with other ministries; here's what our budget now requires." And so on, in constant adjustment and adaptation.

LET MEASUREMENTS AND CONTROLS SERVE CORE WORKERS

Focus on results and outcomes, not behaviors and styles. We saw this principle clearly in setting up a culture of trust. Trust releases our need for control and compliance; again, peer reviews are often more trustworthy than reviews from superiors. We also talked about benchmarking from successful ministries elsewhere so the measurements are "real" (as objective as possible) in relation to the vision and goals.

SUPPORT LOCAL FLAVOR AND LOCAL SOLUTIONS

Don't demand any form of superficial consistency among groups in terms of how they "look" or how they tackle their work. Ministry teams should be able to express unique personalities and let their approaches and methods flow outward. Because teams are capable of crafting their styles according to the particular passions, talents, and personalities among them, diverse teams will exist within one ministry or organization. As a good steward, you let that happen *and* you enjoy it.

DEMAND A PROMISE

If such partnership is going to work, then ownership and responsibility must be shouldered by those working with the leaders (the staff, volunteers, members, etc.). In effect, people must promise to exercise self-discipline to stretch toward goals and expectations they've jointly established.

When these principles take hold, layleaders and staff members can *feel* the freedom and responsibility blossoming in their midst. What empowerment! What joy to work in such a place! Peter Block suggests that our choice to introduce *and retain* this kind of stewardship calls us to create a new contract, or covenant, with those we lead.

Choosing stewardship is the choice to say no to others' desire for you to claim control and in exchange offer them protection. Choosing stewardship is our choice to be accountable while supporting freedom in ourselves and others. This is a risky choice and comes packaged in more anxiety than we had bargained for. This choice for accountability and freedom is the essence of entrepreneurial spirit. It forms the basis for the social contract essential to ownership and responsibility at every level of our organization.[4]

Are you willing to embrace this "risky choice," this contract with the people you're leading? Before we view this leader-volunteer agreement more closely, consider an example in one of the ministries I consulted.

The church had two associate pastors with markedly different styles. At first, both appeared to be very successful, in light of the vitality in their ministries. Over time, though, I saw a big contrast. One of them had gathered many teams around him but wouldn't let go of tight control; he directed every detail of process, style, and method. People went along with his authority for a while, but eventually became exhausted by his need for them to do things his way. Slowly those ministries began to fizzle, until they were discontinued or assigned to others. He'd enjoyed a long tenure at the church, but his role diminished drastically, down to extremely limited authority.

The other associate followed many of the good steward leadership principles outlined above. This was initially difficult for her, and many of the staff accused her of abdicating responsibility because she facilitated the freedom of those she entrusted with the ministry. She responded encouragingly to the styles, processes, methods, and recommendations of team members, offering support and coaching according to their needs. She believed that accountability and freedom could go hand in hand.

I saw this with my own eyes: Her ministries blossomed, multiplied, and expanded during the same period when her controlling colleague watched his ministries dry up. More impressive to me was that, on this particular staff, she'd been given the least-developed part of the ministry when she started, yet she ultimately oversaw more ministry than almost any other department head. The people around her reveled in their empowerment, responsibility, skill development, and the fact that they were trusted to do what they did best.

BUILD A NEW CONTRACT

Built within a good stewardship ministry environment is a new social contract/work contract between leadership and those who follow. Peter Block suggests five significant elements for this contract.[5]

(1) CLARIFY THE CORE MISSION OF THE UNIT

In the midst of all our excitement about empowering individuals and teams, let's remember: There are some things only the leaders can do. We can't leave the development of our core mission to volunteers. As leaders, we've been grasped by a vision and tasked with a mission. People look to us to cast that vision, to inspire them with its excellence, and to show them how, ultimately, it renders obedience to God. At the least, therefore, we must define and clarify the scope of the ministry and the span of care over which we'll have authority.

(2) DEFINE THE EXPECTED OUTCOMES

Teams need to have some sense of senior leadership's expectations. This can involve the other-ministries benchmarks we've discussed.

(3) CHOOSE A STRUCTURE THAT FITS THE SITUATION

Customizing is a good thing! See the big picture, then form your ministry for effectiveness in a particular setting and situation. You're building something, and as with any worthy architectural project, *form follows function*. Once the mission, span of care, and expectations have been outlined, senior leadership can work with layleaders and staff to put together a structure that makes sense for the here and now.

(4) DEFINE THE PARTNERSHIP PRINCIPLES

Does everyone know how the senior leaders and the ministry teams or departments are supposed to relate? You can clearly define this in your contract, or you can let people figure it out for themselves ... eventually ... hopefully. (Guess which approach is best.)

Actually, many special agreements can exist between leaders and those who follow. Some will reflect the organization's agreed-upon values. Others will simply name ways of staying accountable or detail how new resources may get channeled to a particular ministry team or staff group. Think through what relational principles need clear articulation, then state them regularly.

(5) FOCUS ATTENTION IN THE RIGHT PLACES

Upfront and ongoing senior leadership will steer the attention of various teams to opportunities or difficulties they see in the congregation or organization. The focus will change over time as leaders keep experimenting with how ministries might redirect their efforts for greater effectiveness. The goal is not to dictate answers to the ministries but to direct the teams to the right questions or problems for their creative responses.

With these building blocks in mind, consider the sample covenant or "contract planner" below. If you like, you could use it as a basic template for creating the agreement between senior leadership and ministry teams. Some organizations like to use a written form like this one, while others use the items simply as a checklist to make sure they've talked about all the important issues to be ironed out among the various functions of leadership.

MINISTRY TEAM NAME:

- Core mission of this team:

- Expected outcomes this year:

- Selected structure (currently):

PARTNERSHIP PRINCIPLES

- Core organizational values and what they mean:

- Guidelines to follow from senior leadership:

- Span of care (currently):

▪ Ways of staying accountable:

▪ How this team will communicate with senior leadership and integrate with other teams:

▪ Resources the team needs now and how it can later ask for additional or different resources:

To return to our body analogy one final time, we might say that the type of stewardship we've described simply treats people as adults rather than children. When children are small, they need a lot of direction, monitoring, and control; if they don't have these, they can easily harm themselves or others. As they grow up, they can take on more freedom and accountability. The whole point of the parenting process is to create independent and functioning adults who will regulate their own lives.

When organizations try to control people rather than work within the type of contract described above, they begin to regress and act in childish ways. I observed this while consulting a large organization in Minneapolis. The CEO was so focused on having the organization serve him, so intent on controlling employees, that the many mature and competent people around him literally regressed in their behaviors whenever he walked into the room. This is not honoring to the human spirit, and it certainly isn't God's plan for adults to be treated as children.

Which brings us to our pivotal question: "Who are you here to serve?" If you assume (consciously or otherwise) that the organization exists to serve you, you can hardly create an environment of stewardship and shared ownership. Why bypass that blessing? If you're wisely stewarding your organization, holding in trust the assignments it's been given, you'll create an environment of excitement, love, encouragement, peace . . . and even fun! People in your ministry will look forward to fulfilling their responsibilities and reaching the goals you've all designed. They'll know they're accomplishing something great in the kingdom, and they'll feel pleased with their unique contributions.

In fact, you'll all look forward to the time when you will each stand before your Lord, feel His warm smile upon your face, and hear: "Well done, good and faithful servant; enter into My joy." After all, Christ-based leadership does one thing very well: It ultimately brings pleasure to Christ himself.

FOR REFLECTION

Use this space to write down your reflections, reactions, insights, and responses to this chapter and its central question.

Who am I here to serve?

SELECTIVE BIBLIOGRAPHY

Adizes, Ichak. *Corporate Lifecycles.* Englewood Cliffs, NJ: Prentice Hall, 1988.

Barna, George. *Grow Your Church From the Outside In.* Ventura, CA: Regal Books, 2002.

Block, Peter. *Stewardship: Choosing Service Over Self-Interest.* San Francisco: Berrett-Koehler Publishers, 1996.

Buckingham, Marcus. *First, Break All the Rules: What the World's Greatest Managers Do Differently.* New York: Simon & Schuster, 1999.

Buckingham, Marcus, and Donald O. Clifton. *Now, Discover Your Strengths.* New York: Free Press, 2001.

Collins, Jim. *Good to Great: Why Some Companies Make the Leap and Others Don't.* New York: HarperCollins, 2001.

Collins, Jim, with Jerry Porras. *Built to Last: Successful Habits of Vision Companies.* New York: HarperCollins, 1994.

Ghoshal, Sumantra, and Christopher A. Bartlett. *The Individualized Corporation: A Fundamentally New Approach to Management.* New York: HarperCollins, 1999.

Hollender, Jeffrey, with Stephen Fenichell. *What Matters Most: How a Small Group of Pioneers Is Teaching Social Responsibility to Big*

Business and Why Big Business Is Listening. New York: Basic Books, 2004.

Kise, Jane A. G. *Finding and Following God's Will.* Minneapolis: Bethany House, 2005.

Kise, Jane A. G., and David Stark. *Life Directions.* Minneapolis: Bethany House, 1999.

Kise, Jane A. G., David Stark, and Sandra Krebs Hirsh. *LifeKeys: Discover Who You Are.* Minneapolis: Bethany House, revised edition, 2005.

Kiuchi, Tachi, and Bill Shireman. *What We Learned in the Rainforest: Business Lessons From Nature.* San Francisco: Berrett-Koehler Publishers, Inc., 2002.

Lencioni, Patrick M. *Overcoming the Five Dysfunctions of a Team: A Field Guide for Leaders, Managers, and Facilitators.* San Francisco: Jossey-Bass Publishers, 2005.

Moore, James F. *The Death of Competition, Leadership, and Strategy in the Age of Business Ecosystems.* New York: HarperCollins, 1997.

O'Toole, James. *Leading Change: Overcoming the Ideology of Comfort and the Tyranny of Custom.* San Francisco: Jossey-Bass Publishers, 1995.

Parker, Glenn. *Cross-Functional Teams: Working With Allies, Enemies, and Other Strangers.* San Francisco: Jossey-Bass Publishers, 2002.

Simonsen, Peggy. *Promoting a Developmental Culture in Your Organization: Using Career Development As a Change Agent. Mountain View, CA: Davies-Black Publishing, 1997.*

Snyder, Howard A. The Community of the King. Downers Grove, IL: InterVarsity Press, 1997.

Stevens, R. Paul. *Liberating the Laity,* Downers Grove, IL: InterVarsity Press, 1985.

Toffler, Alvin. *The Third Wave.* New York: Bantam Books, 1984.

Wuthnow, Robert. *After Heaven: Spirituality in America Since the 1950s.* Berkeley: University of California Press, 1998.

Zook, Chris. *Beyond the Core: Expanding Your Market Without Abandoning Your Roots.* Cambridge, MA: Harvard Business School Press, 2004.

Zook, Chris, with James Allen. *Profit From the Core: Growth Strategy in an Era of Turbulence.* Cambridge, MA: Harvard Business School Press, 2001.

ENDNOTES

INTRODUCTION

1. Alvin Toffler, *The Third Wave* (New York: Bantam Books, 1984).

2. James O'Toole, *Leading Change: Overcoming the Ideology of Comfort and the Tyranny of Custom* (San Francisco: Jossey-Bass Publishers, 1995), 87.

3. Ibid., 99.

4. Alvin Toffler, *The Third Wave*, 133.

5. James O'Toole, *Leading Change*, 253.

6. Jeffrey Hollender with Stephen Fenichell, *What Matters Most: How a Small Group of Pioneers Is Teaching Social Responsibility to Big Business and Why Big Business Is Listening* (New York: Basic Books, 2004), 264.

CHAPTER ONE

1. Jim Collins, *Good to Great: Why Some Companies Make the Leap and Others Don't* (New York: HarperCollins, 2001), 39. Used by permission.

2. Frederick Buechner, *The Magnificent Defeat* (New York: HarperCollins, 1985).

CHAPTER TWO

1. Jane A. G. Kise and David Stark, *Life Directions* (Minneapolis: Bethany House, 1999), 29, 55, 89, 125.

2. Henri J. M. Nouwen, *Clowning in Rome: Reflections on Solitiude, Celibacy, Prayer, and Contemplation* (New York: Doubleday, 1979), 70–71.

3. Ronald Rolheiser, *The Holy Longing* (New York: Random House, 1999), 223, 225.

4. Katherine Dyckman and L. Patrick Carroll, *Inviting the Mystic, Supporting the Prophet* (New York: Paulist Press, 1981).

5. Jane A. G. Kise, *Finding and Following God's Will* (Minneapolis: Bethany House, 2005).

6. Jim Collins, with Jerry Porras, *Built to Last: Successful Habits of Vision Companies* (New York: HarperCollins, 1994).

CHAPTER THREE

1. Joachim Jeremias, *Jerusalem in the Time of Jesus* (Minneapolis: Fortress Press, 1969), 196–97.

2. Sumantra Ghoshal and Christopher A. Bartlett, *The Individualized Corporation: A Fundamentally New Approach to Management* (New York: HarperCollins, 1999).

3. Ibid.

4. Ibid.

5. Ibid., 98.

6. Ibid., 67.

CHAPTER FOUR

1. James Houston, *The Transforming Power of Prayer*, quoted in *Christianity Today* (April 29, 1996).

2. R. Paul Stevens, *Liberating the Laity* (Downers Grove, IL: InterVarsity Press, 1985), 50.

3. Ibid., 111–21.

4. James Hind, in *Life* magazine, quoted in *New Man* (March-April 1995).

CHAPTER FIVE

1. *www.coolillusions.com.* Gallery #1, Casale Media, Invisible Triangle.

2. Ibid., Jazz Lady.

3. Glenn Parker, *Cross-Functional Teams: Working With Allies, Enemies, and Other Strangers* (San Francisco: Jossey-Bass Publishers, 2002), 5.

CHAPTER SIX

1. Jim Collins, *Good to Great,* 160.

2. Jim Collins, *Good to Great.*

3. See text below on "Hedgehog Concept."

CHAPTER SEVEN

1. Marcus Buckingham, *First, Break All the Rules: What the World's Greatest Managers Do Differently* (New York: Simon & Schuster, 1999), 43–48. Used by permission.

2. Marcus Buckingham and Donald O. Clifton, *Now, Discover Your Strengths* (New York: Free Press, 2001), 6–7.

3. Ibid., 5.

4. Ibid.

5. One tool that has helped churches with these job descriptions is the book *LifeKeys,* which helps to empower both lay volunteers and paid staff in their gifts, talents, and passions. (Jane A. G. Kise, David Stark, and Sandra Krebs Hirsh [Minneapolis: Bethany House, 1996], revised in 2005 and titled *LifeKeys: Discover Who You Are.*)

6. Peggy Simonsen, *Promoting a Developmental Culture in Your Organization: Using Career Development As a Change Agent* (Mountain View, CA: Davies-Black Publishing, 1997), 221.

7. C. S. Lewis, *The Four Loves* (New York: Harvest Books, 1971), 166.

8. Ibid.

CHAPTER EIGHT

1. James S. Hewett, *Illustrations Unlimited* (Wheaton, IL: Tyndale House, 1988), 123.

2. Patrick M. Lencioni, *Overcoming the Five Dysfunctions of a Team: A Field Guide for Leaders, Managers, and Facilitators* (San Francisco: Jossey-Bass Publishers, 2005), 4.

3. Ibid.

4. David Augsburger, *Caring Enough to Confront* (Ventura, CA.: Regal Books, 1974).

5. Cited in James S. Hewett, *Illustrations Unlimited* (Wheaton, IL: Tyndale House, 1972), 124.

CHAPTER NINE

1. Howard A. Snyder, *The Community of the King* (Downers Grove, IL: InterVarsity Press, 1977), 139.

2. Sumantra Ghoshal and Christopher A. Bartlett, *The Individualized Corporation: A Fundamentally New Approach to Management* (New York: HarperBusiness, 1999), 213.

3. Ibid., 191.

4. Howard A. Snyder, *The Community of the King*, 39.

CHAPTER TEN

1. Ichak Adizes, *Corporate Lifecycles* (Englewood Cliffs, NJ: Prentice Hall, 1988), 4.

2. Ibid., 11–60.

CHAPTER ELEVEN

1. Tachi Kiuchi and Bill Shireman, *What We Learned in the Rainforest: Business Lessons From Nature* (San Francisco: Berrett-Koehler Publishers, Inc., 2002), 59.

2. *www.afrol.com/Categories/Environment/index_mangroves.htm*

3. James F. Moore, *The Death of Competition, Leadership, and Strategy in the Age of Business Ecosystems* (New York: HarperCollins, 1997), 88.

4. George Barna, *Grow Your Church From the Outside In* (Ventura, CA: Regal Books, 2002), 48.

5. Ibid., 84.

6. Robert Wuthnow, *After Heaven: Spirituality in America Since the 1950s* (Berkeley: University of California Press, 1998), 75.

7. *Publisher's Weekly* review at *amazon.com*.

8. Chris Zook, with James Allen, *Profit From the Core: Growth Strategy in an Era of Turbulence* (Cambridge, MA: Harvard Business School Press, 2001), 25.

9. Ibid., 74.

10. George Barna, *Grow Your Church From the Outside In,* 112–13.

11. Tachi Kiuchi and Bill Shireman, *What We Learned in the Rainforest,* 63.

12. James F. Moore, *The Death of Competition, Leadership, and Strategy in the Age of Business Ecosystems,* 142.

CHAPTER TWELVE

1. Peter Block, *Stewardship: Choosing Service Over Self-Interest* (San Francisco: Berrett-Koehler Publishers, 1996), 41.

2. Ibid., 64–68.

3. Ibid., 84.

4. Ibid.

5. Ibid., 69–74.